Shine While You Dine

"Business Dining Etiquette for the Virtual Age"

Manners Matter,
Courtesy Counts!

RA Sh

Robert A. Shutt

authorHOUSE®

AuthorHouse™
1663 Liberty Drive
Bloomington, IN 47403
www.authorhouse.com
Phone: 1-800-839-8640

First published by AuthorHouse 5/3/2011

ISBN: 978-1-4567-1329-4 (sc)
ISBN: 978-1-4567-1330-0 (e)

Library of Congress Control Number: 2010918966

Printed in the United States of America

Any people depicted in stock imagery provided by Thinkstock are models, and such images are being used for illustrative purposes only.
Certain stock imagery © Thinkstock.

This book is printed on acid-free paper.

Acknowledgements

Shine While You Dine is dedicated to those who cared enough to teach me the importance of appropriate behavior, most notably my parents and grandparents. It is also dedicated to all of my clients who invite me to entertain and educate audiences throughout the land. I am also grateful to Dr. Carole Gustitas who first invited me to speak on this topic and Abigail Mac Fadden who enhanced the quality of this work with her editing skills. Special thanks go to my son Mackinaw who inspires me daily with his creative intellect and generous heart. Finally, I am indebted to Lynne Marie who made good work great.

Table of Contents

Welcome

Hello and welcome to *Shine While You Dine*, a book intended to help you "shine through" by mastering the seemingly complicated nuances of business dining etiquette. In this book, you will discover the genuine value dining etiquette adds to your professional persona. (Hint: It is not so you can show off your dexterity with the butter spreader.) You will come to understand how this skill—universal to all professions—is an integral part of our culture: past, present, and future. Finally, and most importantly, you will learn three foundations, two guiding principles, and one single objective that make it easy to follow the numerous rules, guidelines, and behaviors outlined in this book.

This approach makes etiquette mastery as easy as one-two-three. Stay focused on your one single objective, use the two guiding principles to determine what behavior would be most suitable at any time and in any situation, and you will naturally adhere to the three foundations of all appropriate behavior. This approach also helps you negotiate any cultural, geographic, or formality nuances you might encounter.

The guidelines that I provide are purposefully conservative and formal. They are also most specific to the Northeast region of the United States and Canada. Adhering to the guiding principles will enable you to relax when your actions are too formal. Adhering to the foundations will enable you to adjust when cultural or geographic discrepancies occur. This approach is an etiquette elixir!

SECTION ONE:

Preliminaries

Chapter 1

Appropriate Behavior versus Etiquette

Let's begin by dropping the intrinsic pretentiousness created by the word "etiquette". I think it is a poor word to use when discussing this topic since it often repels and frightens people. *"Etiquette,"* they shriek as they flee in terror. *"Not the illogical rules our elders tried to drill into us. What's next—the wonderful world of land-line telephones and the typewriter?"* Please, let the shrieking and fleeing stop right now. Etiquette is just a snazzy word that means "the manners, rules, behaviors, and ceremonies conventionally accepted or required in social, professional, or official life". To state it directly, etiquette is appropriate behavior.

Wherever you go and whatever you do, rules of appropriate behavior surround you. Did you drive to work today? Traffic laws are rules of appropriate behavior. Did you use your cell phone today? Seeking a private area to speak is a rule of appropriate behavior. Have you played golf recently? Letting the person with the lowest score on the previous hole tee-off first is a rule of appropriate behavior. Have you flown lately? Deplaning row-by-row is a rule of appropriate behavior. In this book, we examine the rules of appropriate behavior followed at a so-called "business" meal. This examination leads to two obvious questions: why does it matter and what is a so-called "business" meal?

Chapter 2

Why It Matters

There are a number of reasons appropriate behavior matters. One reason is **appropriate behavior eliminates distractions**—distractions caused by inappropriate behavior. When someone tailgates us while driving, speaks on his cell phone at a movie theatre, or walks in front of our putting line on the golf course, we notice.

Think about it. Try to recall a time when someone behaved poorly in your presence. You were aware of the inappropriate behavior so much so that you remember it now. Chances are you also remember the individual who behaved so poorly. You might even be able to picture that person in your head right now. Consider this example.

Some years ago, I was flying to a speaking engagement at a national conference. As I boarded the commuter jet, I was overwhelmed with the odor of pepperoni and onion. One of the passengers had brought a full-size pizza on the plane. She looked to be a businessperson and was seated across the aisle and two rows behind me. I saw that the passenger seated next to her, who did not seem to be traveling with her, had lost the use of her tray table; the pizza box was that big. During the flight, I could hear her noisily enjoying a slice or two. I did not hear her offer any to her neighbor. When the plane landed and we arrived at our gate, the bell rang to signal that we were free to exit our seats. She stood up immediately and rushed to the front of the plane ahead of all the other passengers, including me. During this exodus, she used the pizza box to block the aisle from all who thought of exiting their seat. She was nine rows back, yet departed first. I can still see her face clearly in my head and will remember her and her poor behavior forever, as will most of the passengers on that flight.

I know this to be true because this bad behavior had major repercussions. This woman had not understood the second reason why appropriate behavior matters—**your organization is judged by your behavior**. This is a somewhat subtle point at times because we don't always appreciate when we might be representing our organization. Certainly, this businessperson did not.

As mentioned, I was flying to speak at a national convention. This person was flying to the same convention. She was a vendor at the convention's trade show. Sadly, her inappropriate behavior on the plane led to an unsuccessful trip. She appeared bewildered why attendance at her booth was light for she presented a polished persona at the convention, but I knew why. Not only had I been on the plane, I had overheard the hushed conversations on the convention floor about her pizza faux pas. She had not realized that she was representing her organization on the plane as well as on the convention floor.

Although the above reasons are relatively subtle, it does not belittle their importance. Still some may think these reasons aren't good enough to worry about business dining etiquette. If so, continue reading.

The most obvious reason (and for many the most important reason) that appropriate behavior matters is that **you are judged by your behavior**. But to what degree? The quick answer is to a higher degree than you ever imagined.

Oft-quoted research suggests that as much as 85% of your career success may be a result of your interpersonal skills. *"Why is that?"* you continue to ask.

"Because interpersonal skills determine your ability to present yourself and your ideas effectively to people," I patiently answer. Professionals have understood this fact for at least 5,000 years. We know this because of a man named Ptahhotep.

Ptahhotep lived around 3,000 BC and was an assistant to a high priest in ancient Egypt. His tomb contains what may be the oldest written (in hieroglyphics) business etiquette guideline. The guideline says that when sitting with your superiors, laugh when they laugh. This is still good advice, although I would amend it a bit by adding that you shouldn't laugh if it is politically incorrect or inappropriate to the situation.

Why It Matters
1. Appropriate behavior eliminates distractions.
2. Your organization is judged by your behavior.
3. You are judged by your behavior.
4. Appropriate behavior strongly influences career success.

This seemingly innocuous piece of advice reveals the subtle power of appropriate behavior. Our behavior may communicate more than we think it does. Laughing when your superior laughs may suggest that you can see things from his perspective which is a quality most superiors appreciate.

This doesn't mean superiors want to be surrounded by "yes" people who blindly agree with whatever they say,

although to be honest some do. The most effective superiors appreciate people who can tactfully disagree and
offer alternative ideas and thoughts, especially when doing
so after listening to and reflecting upon their superior's
perspective. Laughing when your superior laughs suggests
you may possess this trait.

Appropriate behavior clearly matters because your **interpersonal skills contribute to your career success**.
I fully appreciated the value of interpersonal skills during
my 20-year career as an administrator, director, and manager in the retail, higher education, and hospitality fields.
I interviewed and hired hundreds of people over the years
for a broad range of positions. I would usually start with
up to 200 candidates for a single position, so the first step
was to review their cover letters and resumes. I discarded
those applicants who did not meet my educational and/
or experience parameters as well as those applicants who
did not know how to write and present these documents.
(Note to students: use the resources offered by your career
services department.) This usually left me with about 15 or
so applicants. I would then review references, speak with
previous employers, and so on. Soon I would have a pool
of five or six final candidates I would invite for a personal
interview.

Truth be told, these interviews were a bit of a charade
since I knew that every single final candidate could perform
the job, at least the functional or technical aspect of it. I
knew this because of the research I had done regarding
their education, experience, and references. Confirming this
was NOT the purpose of the interview. All the management
candidates could manage; all the accountant candidates
could prepare an income statement; all the custodians could
clean a toilet. Therefore, the real purpose of the interview

was to see who would be the best interpersonal fit for my organization, not to see who could do the functions of the job. The interviews answered these questions for me:

- Who would work best with me?
- Who would work best with my customers?
- Who would fit in best with my staff?
- Who would best communicate ideas and thoughts without distraction?
- Whose behavior would best mirror the culture of my organization?

All questions were answered by their ability to behave appropriately. For these reasons and so many more, appropriate behavior—business dining etiquette—matters. Now let's get to our second question: what is a "business meal"?

Chapter 3

What Is a So-called "Business" Meal?

You should adhere to the rules of dining etiquette whenever you eat in the company of others. Meals occur in one of two etiquette environments. Knowing which environment you are in will determine which guidelines you follow. The behavioral distinctions are sometimes subtle, so I suggest you pre-determine your etiquette environment before you arrive. It's easy to do. Ask yourself, *"What is the main purpose of the meal?"*

Most meals fall under the umbrella of **social dining** where social etiquette rules apply. The main purpose of a social meal is usually one of the two c's: companionship or cuisine. When you eat with family, friends, or the hottie from your pottery class, you are dining for companionship. The main reason you share the meal is so you can relish in the camaraderie of their company. When you decide to taste-test the new Thai restaurant or re-investigate a familiar Italian restaurant, you are dining for cuisine. The main reason you share the meal is so you can savor the culinary arts with others. When you gather for your Thanksgiving feast, you are enjoying both companionship and cuisine.

Our focus will be on **business** dining, the so-called "business meal". I define such a meal as **a food and/or beverage event you attend that may have an impact on your career now or in the future**. This is true of anyone on any career path. I actually dislike using the term "business" dining because it implies that these guidelines apply only to people in traditional business careers. You know: accounting, finance, sales, and so on. This is not an accurate assumption. These guidelines can help anyone: artists, educators, scientists, and techies too. I prefer the phrase **professional dining etiquette** as it more accurately reflects this fact because **these guidelines can help anyone in any profession.** Whether you're an artist or an accountant, if the people you dine with can enhance your career, you are attending a so-called "business meal".

The main purpose at a **professional** dining meal is the relationship you are creating, maintaining, or enhancing. Job interviews, sales discussions, and partnership dialogues are examples of such a professional dining meal. Another common situation for a professional dining meal includes a "working lunch". Most people recognize these types of business meals. However, there is another professional dining situation that is often missed by even the most experienced professional.

Food and/or beverage events you attend where you may be acting as a representative of your organization, whether you intend to or not, are also business meals. Conferences, holiday parties, golf outings, and company picnics are such business meals. Too often people think of these events as social outings and view them as an opportunity to show off their partying skills. They beckon back to college or high school and channel their inner late adolescent persona. This is a bad idea! Such thinking has sabotaged many a career. Think of these events as business meetings or business meals and act accordingly. You never know when someone is evaluating your company by your behavior. I almost learned this the hard way.

For many years, I worked an hour away from my home. To get to work, I had to pass through a mountain range which made the two communities more distinct than you might imagine. The town where I worked was in the Commonwealth of Pennsylvania; I lived in upstate New York. When I was at work, I never saw people from home. While at home, I never saw people from work. As a result, I got a little lazy with some personal habits like shaving my face during the weekend.

When I woke on a Saturday or Sunday, I liked to linger in my pajamas, enjoy a cup of coffee, grow a little bristle, and cherish the unique look of my bed-head. What did I care? No one from work would see me and my neighbors and family already loved me, so they were not likely to judge me too harshly. I would occasionally need some bread or a little cream for my coffee. A little mom-and-pop grocery store was located about one mile down the road, so I would jump on my bicycle or hop in my car and go down for supplies without a glance in the mirror. If someone saw me there and judged me a slob, so be it. They would only be judging Robert from the neighborhood.

I eventually left this out-of-state position to work for a local company. A few months after being hired, the company opened a branch office one and a half miles from my home and a half-mile from the local mom-and-pop. A week or so after the grand opening, we needed bread on a Sunday morning. My initial thought was to run right down to the store. As I grabbed my car keys, I happened to see my reflection in the mirror; it was not a pleasant sight. My bed-head was raging and I had a two-day beard. (I can grow whiskers quickly.) I had slept in a torn tee shirt that had the logo of a bar on it. My gym shorts were mismatched and equally tattered. I thought, "What if I run into someone *from work? Do I want to look like this?" I decided I did not, so I shaved, combed my hair, and changed clothes.*

Sure enough, while waiting at the check-out counter, a neighbor I knew casually approached me. He asked if I was associated with the newly opened branch and I said that I was. He told me that he had heard about a new product being offered. I told him what I knew about it. As he left the store he said, "Thanks, Robert. It was good to see you. You're looking good." Three days later, he purchased our product.

As my experience illustrates, the distinction between a business and social meal is sometimes blurry. For example, when you share lunch with co-workers from the office, social rules usually apply if the agenda is companionship or cuisine. If it is a working lunch, business rules apply. My advice is to always err on the side of business, so if you're not sure, assume business rules apply. After all, we are talking about your career here.

Chapter 4

Foundations and Focused
First Impressions

People have known the value of appropriate behavior for at least 5,000 years as proved by Ptahhotep. (See Chapter 2: Why It Matters.) *"But,"* you may skeptically say, *"what does ancient Egypt have to do with modern times?"* Aside from the subtleties illustrated by Ptahhotep's suggestion, maybe not all that much. I mean we no longer bury treasures with our dead leaders as they did. It turns out that wasn't such a good idea unless your goal was to give treasure hunters, looters, and thieves an obvious target. We also no longer believe a sacred beetle (called a scarab) pushes the sun across the sky as they reputedly did. Science has yet to find evidence of this; there are no holy beetle droppings in space. Don't get me wrong—Ancient Egypt is a fascinating civilization to study. I admire and respect them greatly. In some ways, they had superior knowledge to ours. I'm just acknowledging that a 5,000 year old reference from an ancient civilization may seem irrelevant.

Let's look at a more germane reference—none other than George Washington, the acclaimed "Father of our Country". When George Washington was 14 or 15 years old, he took out his trusty quill pen, dipped it in his ink well, and wrote out 110 "Rules of Civility and Decent Behavior". These guidelines remain in print and are mostly applicable even to this day. He followed these rules throughout his life and they served him well in a variety of professions including surveyor, planter, soldier, or politician. Consequently, I think of George Washington as the "Father of Civility" too.

I believe Washington's appreciation for appropriate behavior made him the ideal choice to be the first President in part because he understood that **he represented the organization with which he was associated**. In his case, the organization was the new nation, the United States of America. He practiced this principle so well that even today, centuries after he served as president, his image remains one of most recognized icons of the nation. Show his picture to anyone on any continent and there is a good chance they will know who he is and what nation he represents. Try that with James Buchanan or Chester Arthur.

I mention Washington before we get to the nuances of dining behavior because he also understood the importance of first impressions. He wrote three rules that I urge you to practice even before the meal begins. Remember he wrote these more than 250 years ago so we may need to revise them just a bit. Nonetheless, he said:

- *"Sit not when others stand."*
- *"Sleep not when others speak."*
- *"When another speaks, be attentive yourself and disturb not the audience."*

These are important rules to follow because they confirm that you understand the three foundations of all appropriate behavior. A closer look reveals how these behaviors can help create a positive first impression.

Clients often ask me, *"What is the most common business etiquette faux pas you see?"* The most common error

I witness is when people ignore Washington's rule: sit not when others stand. This happens in a variety of situations; however, the most common time for this error to occur is when first impressions are established during introductions. This is why I have updated Washington's guideline and urge you to **rise to meet and greet people**.

Whenever there is an introduction and one person is standing, all involved should stand too. This is true when you introduce yourself, when someone introduces himself to you, and when someone introduces others to you. This also applies whenever you greet someone in your office, at the table, etc. If seated, you should always rise to meet or greet someone who is standing, just as George suggests.

Respect the hierarchy is the foundation this action confirms. When you rise to meet or greet someone, you show that you understand the hierarchy of the situation. Standing to shake hands says that there is no one and nothing more important to you at this time than this person. Whereas if you remain seated, you risk saying, *"It is kind of nice to meet you; however, my physical comfort is a little more important to me at this time, so I will remain seated."*

A side note to this behavior concerns the order of intro-ductions. The guideline is simple; you say the name of the most important person first. This action ensures that you respect the hierarchy.

"Ms. Department Head," you say, *"I'd like you to meet Mr. Employee."*

Also remember with business introductions, it is the organizational hierarchy that dictates importance, not gen-der. (See Chapter 13: Business Versus Social Etiquette.)

Therefore, the customer or client is the most important person. For example:

"Mr. CEO," you say, "I'd like you to meet Ms. Middle Manager."
"Ms. Customer," you say, "Let me introduce Mr. CEO."

A final introduction tip is to use titles: Dr., Mr., Mrs., the Honorable, etc. Use titles even when the person you are introducing allows you to call him by his first name. It's up to him to decide who else is granted that privilege; it is not up to you. For example:

You are walking down the hall with your customer, Kirk Gibson, and you run into Robert Arthur, who is the CEO. You call him Robert. You want to introduce them.
"Robert, it's good to see you," you say in greeting. Then you restart. "Mr. Gibson, I would like you to meet Mr. Arthur, our company CEO."

After they shake, you may continue:

"Mr. Gibson is one of the largest purchasers of our innovative new widget wizard. He's here to tour the production facilities. Mr. Arthur has been our CEO for the past three years and our production efficiency is at an all time high."

This courteous sharing of background information facilitates any conversation they might engage in later when you are no longer around.

An additional way to make a positive first impression (while avoiding a common mistake) is to remember another of Washington's rules: sleep not when others speak. This one takes a little explaining since most of you realize that falling asleep during a business meal is not a particularly wise move. When I first read this rule, I thought to myself, *"Did he really have to write that one down?"* It seems like a no-brainer, at least in today's world. Upon reflection, I realized that Washington did not live in our world, as two aspects of his daily life were vastly different from ours.

Travel was very different. Our three-hour drive could be a nine-day journey in Washington's time. Our bucket seat is encased in an air-conditioned automobile moving over a well-maintained paved highway; his was a hard leather saddle strapped atop a sweaty horse jostling over an uneven, muddy pathway. Our pit stop for a cappuccino and gas was evening-after-evening spent at a drover's inn grooming, feeding, and boarding the horse. We arrive refreshed whereas they arrived exhausted. Communication was also very different. Orators in Washington's time spoke for hours and sometimes days at a time. We cherish the five-second sound byte. Consequently, sleeping while others spoke was a relatively common occurrence.

Times have changed but the importance of the second foundation has not. **Focus on a single agenda** is the foundation this action confirms. Focus your actions, words, and behavior on the agenda connected to the person (or people) with you. When you fall asleep, your focus is clearly elsewhere.

I have modernized this rule too and believe Washington would now urge us to **cell not, text not, PDA not when another speaks**. Any of these actions communicate the same message as falling asleep: something or someone else is more important than the people (or person) with you. So please turn these devices off and focus on the people with you.

As a side note, this is the most common faux pas reported to me by others, specifically by executives and managers.

Their concern is that inappropriate use of the cell phone, PDA, etc. conveys a lack of focus which greatly troubles them. Think about it—in many ways it is a lot like sleeping in Washington's time. When you text message, check your appointments, use your cell, listen to music, or nap while in the company of another (or others), you risk sending a message that says, *"My focus is on this message, this appointment, this call, this music, this nap. It is NOT on you."*

The most universal foundation is courtesy. **Courtesy** is an awareness of the impact your behavior, actions, and words have upon the people you are with as well as those in your proximity. Willingly, generously, and voluntarily providing something needed by another personifies courtesy. Washington expressed this in another rule: when another speaks, be attentive yourself and disturb not the audience. Here is my modern version: **keep your side conversations quiet and to a minimum during a meeting, speech, presentation, or seminar.**

Foundations of Appropriate Behavior

Focus on a single agenda: Cell not, text not, PDA not when another speaks.

Respect the hierarchy: Rise to greet and meet

Courtesy, an awareness of the impact your behavior, actions, and words have upon the people you are with as well as those in your proximity: Keep your side conversations quiet and to a minimum, during a meeting, speech, presentation, or seminar.

We have all experienced those moments when we are uninvolved, disengaged, disinterested, or downright bored during a meeting, speech, presentation, or seminar. We assume others around us feel the same way so we engage them in conversation which is discourteous. It is discourteous to those whom you engage in conversation as they may prefer to remain attentive. It is discourteous to whoever has the floor as it can disrupt the quality of her delivery. It is discourteous to those seated around or near you as your side conversation is distracting and may reduce their ability to remain attentive.

We will close with another of George Washington's rules of civility: kill no vermin as fleas, lice, ticks, and such in the sight of others. Times have changed as this is no longer a vital concern. Thankfully, few of us need to kill vermin, fleas, lice, or ticks while pursuing our professional goals, at least not with the frequency experienced during Washington's time. Still, I include this rule because it illustrates some key points.

One key point is that it addresses the importance of discretion. The rule remains relevant because of this essential element. The management dictum to "reprimand in private, praise in public" reflects this principle as well. The goal in both scenarios (reprimanding and critter killing in private) is to avoid embarrassing another. Letting the world know about vermin, fleas, lice, or ticks that require elimination may be as embarrassing as letting the world know about performance that requires improvement. All George is saying is to go ahead and kill them but do so discretely.

This rule also reiterates the universality of the three foundations. Eliminating unwanted visitors such as vermin, fleas, lice, and ticks is courteous. Elimination also demonstrates that you respect the situational hierarchy; uninvited guests need to make an appointment. Finally, it shows that your focus is on a single agenda—the one associated with the people or person with you and not the activities of a meandering mouse.

The stage is set and the foundations are laid, so let's leave the preliminaries behind and get to the meal where two guiding principles lead the way.

SECTION TWO:

Moving to the Table

Chapter 5

The Single Objective: Let You Shine Through

Successfully negotiating a business meal is easier than most people think. (See Chapter 3: What Is a So-called "Business" Meal?) Too often we get lost in the minutia, and if you seek minutia, etiquette is a rich vein to mine. Which fork do I use? The soup is too hot; how can I cool it? Someone asked me to pass the salt; what do I do?

This book, filled with minutia, will answer these questions and more. Yet I do not encourage you to focus on these rules, guidelines, and behaviors. In fact I discourage it because when you focus on the minutia, your single objective becomes blurry and your objective at such a meal is **to let you shine through** so that you **shine while you dine.**

The idea is simple. The reason you are meeting over a meal is to communicate what is wonderful, unique, or special about you, your organization, or the product or service you represent. Your goal is to create, develop, maintain, or strengthen your relationship(s) with your fellow diner(s). You can only "shine through" when you focus on this goal.

"But," you protest, *"what about all the rules? I don't want to behave inappropriately."* Relax. All you need to remember are the two guiding principles that keep your focus on letting you shine through.

Chapter 6

Guiding Principles: Starting the Meal

The first guiding principle leads you through the start of any meal. It is a principle you learned when you were very young while playing the childhood game **Follow (or be) the Leader.** Obviously, to follow this principle you must first determine who the leader is. Fortunately, in the business world this is relatively easy to do. **The person who does the inviting is the leader.** As such, they get to run the meal. If a group does the inviting, the group is the leader. If you do the inviting, you are the leader. As we will see, the leader can delegate certain duties to others, most often to members of the hospitality staff.

Determining the leader at a business meal is an example of situational hierarchy. Situational hierarchy can super-sede the organizational chart. For example, when meeting someone, he is the most important person in your world, regardless of his title or position. Hence the need to **rise to greet and meet people** (Chapter 4: Foundations and Focused First Impressions). Another example of situational hierarchy is elevator etiquette.

Imagine you work in a twenty-story building. At the end of the day, your CEO gets on the elevator, entering from her top floor office. As the car descends, it slowly fills. You crowd in on the fourth floor (this is early in your career). You arrive at the lobby and the doors open. If you adhered to the organizational hierarchy, everyone in the car would crowd up against the walls and create a path like the parting of the Red Sea to let the CEO exit from the back of the car. Fortunately, we do not follow this guideline as this would be awkward and uncomfortable for all involved. Instead, we follow the rules of elevator etiquette which say that a situational hierarchy exists. In this hierarchy, the person closest to the door exists first regardless of their organizational status.

Business dining is another arena where a situational hierarchy exists. The person who does the inviting is the leader. For this book, I will assume you are the follower (the invitee). When you are the leader (the inviter), switch roles. For now, assume you receive an invitation to a so-called business meal. The invitation could come from an individual and be made by phone call, e-mail, text message, in-person—whatever. It could also come from a group of people, a conference planning committee, your board of directors, and so on. Regardless, **the first thing you do is confirm your plans**.

If you can attend, accept the invitation. If you cannot, decline the invitation. Do not leave them hanging. For formal events, you may receive a written invitation. On it will be the letters *RSVP*. These letters mean to *tell us one way or another what your plans are. Tell us if you are going to attend OR if you are not going to attend.* They do not mean to *tell us only if you plan on coming.* Okay, they actually mean *"Reservations s'il vous plait"* which is French for *"Reservations if you please"*. It must be the "if you please" part that confuses people

---

Two Guiding Principles

1. Follow the Leader.

2. It is about the relationship, the conversation, the business; it is not about the food or the beverage.

---

because it really does mean to *tell us what you plan to do*. This is courtesy-based behavior as anyone who has planned a formal meal can attest. You need to provide a headcount to the caterer or restaurant which can only be done when you know who is or who is not attending.

The leader, by extending the invitation, now has all sorts of decisions to make. As I said, he runs the meal. A good leader delegates and empowers, but not everyone is a good leader, not even when it comes to a meal. The **leader decides where the meal is going to take place and when it will happen**. Ideally, he will consider your preferences and schedule when doing so. If he does not and if you have specific parameters to be considered, you may share this with him beforehand.

Start out subtly and tactfully. *"I would love to join you for lunch next week. Thursday looks good for me,"* is better than, *"I might be able to squeeze you in, but only if it is on Thursday."* If he misses your clue and schedules it for Tuesday, determine how important this meal is to you. If it is more important than the appointment you already have, reschedule the appointment that conflicts. If it is not, politely decline and express your hope that you can a find a mutually agreeable date in the future.

Be subtle and tactful with dietary parameters too. *"Lunch sounds great. I heard that a wonderful new vegetarian restaurant opened down the street,"* is better than, *"Lunch will work. You know I don't eat meat, right?"* Worse case scenario, he misses your clue and picks a steak house. If you are a vegetarian, go anyway. It doesn't mean you have to eat steak. A savvy and attentive leader picks up on tactful clues and plans accordingly. However, regardless of your parameters, the leader determines when and where you dine.

When you accept an invitation, **arrive early**, ideally five to ten minutes before the designated time. Then **wait for the leader to arrive**. Wait in the lobby or by the maitre de's stand if possible. Many restaurants provide chairs for this purpose. If you will be late to a small meal or large event, call the leader or the restaurant and let them know. Call before the scheduled start time. If attending a small meal, offer to reschedule if you will be more than fifteen minutes late.

The leader initiates the move to the dining table so do not go the table before he or she arrives, not even to wait for them. Also, avoid waiting in the lounge or bar. If the lounge or bar is the only option, sit at a table, not at the bar, and order only water. Letting the leader initiate the move to table shows that you respect the situational hierarchy.

This rule holds true at large events too, even when a reception precedes the meal. Too often I see people waltz from the reception area into the dining room before the leader or his representative invites them in. I call this action "staking your claim". You have seen this move before. The crowd is in the reception area, taking advantage of the networking opportunity provided. People are mixing, mingling, creating, and strengthening relationships. Then someone peeks into the dining area and decides that she wants to save a place for herself. Maybe she wants to have good view of the head table or maybe she needs to face east when dining—who knows. She walks in, leans the chair up against the table, or puts her clutch purse on the chair, or drapes her jacket over the back of the chair. Regardless of how she does it, the message she sends is clear. This action says, *"I am the most important person here so I will select my seat before all others. I do not care if the leader, host, or hostess has a specific seat picked out for me!"* If you need to go to your seat before invited to do so, remember to ask permission first. When you do, you are respecting the hierarchy and not staking your claim.

The leader will initiate the move to the table or tables. He may lead or invite you in personally, although typically this duty is delegated to a member of the hospitality staff: maitre de', waitperson, host, etc. Once you arrive at the table, follow **the leader when you select and take your seat**. The leader gets to determine the seating chart even when only two dine.

When dining at a restaurant or private home with only one table in use, pause upon arriving at the table to see if the leader indicates a seating preference. He may use a hand gesture to indicate where you should sit or he may simply select his seat, at which point you may select yours. Stand behind your chair until the leader either sits or says, *"Please be seated."* When you are the leader, try to give the best seat to your guest. It may be the most comfortable or the one with the best view, etc.

When attending a large event, respect place cards and table assignments when used. Sitting elsewhere is discourteous, unfocused, and disrespectful. Moreover, your seat might be next to someone the leader knows will have a positive impact on your career. Imagine that you're an aspiring actor and, unbeknownst to you, have been purposefully seated next to a casting agent. You arrive, find your place card at one table, and see that your friend, Monique, is at another table. You decide, *"What's with the place cards? I want to have fun,"* so you switch your place card with someone at Monique's table. You and Monique see each other once again; someone else gets the part and launches his career.

Usually neither assigned tables nor place cards are

used. Instead, it is an open stampede. The staff opens the doors to the dining area, announces that dinner is about to be served, and the rush is on. Elbows fly, fists flail (even while grasping their reception cocktails), causalities mount, and the "good" seats fill quickly. I suggest an alternative strategy, one that shows you understand the second guiding principle. Remember there are only two. The first guiding principle is to **follow the leader**. The second is that **it is about the relationship, the conversation, the business; it is not about the food or beverage**. Rushing to the table suggests that the food is your focus. Lingering, conversing, and moving to the table while conversing with someone suggests that relationships matter to you more than the food does.

So take your time. Feel free to finish a conversation and let the rush happen. When the rush abates a bit, leave your reception glassware and china in the reception area and enter the dining area. A word of caution—do not wait too long to enter. Arriving at a table after the meal service begins suggests disrespect for the hierarchy. Remember the leader gets to determine when the meal starts so be there when it does.

When you enter the dining room and no assigned tables or place cards are used, strategically select your table. Remember it's about relationships and conversations. Do not pick a table because it is close to the kitchen (so you will be served first), or because it has a nice view, or because is close to the exit. Pick your table because of the people dining at it.

Approach the table and select a chair. If the table has empty seats, stand behind your chair for a minute or two to see if others join you. If they do, you are already standing to greet and/or meet them; rising is not necessary. Once most of the table is full, go ahead and take your seat. If you are seated and someone joins you before the meal service begins, rise to greet or meet him or her, regardless of gender (Chapter 13: Business Versus Social Etiquette).

At meal events associated with conferences and trade shows or at holiday parties and company picnics, try to meet and dine with people you do not see everyday. Divide and conquer, so to speak, as it will enhance the value of the experience for you and your peers. It will also ensure that others don't have to experience what I did a few years back.

I traveled cross-country from upstate New York to California to speak at my first national convention. The night before I presented, I attended the formal kick-off dinner, relishing the networking opportunity. The thought of dining with nine potential clients excited me. First, I attended the reception held before the dinner, practicing my finest networking skills. Then the hospitality staff, serving as representatives of the leaders, announced dinner while opening the doors to a grand ballroom. The rush was on!

I chose to linger a few minutes, closing a conversation first. As the crowd thinned, I placed my appetizer plate and cocktail glass on a bus-tray and entered the dining room. I found a ten-top table that had one empty seat. I didn't recognize any of the other guests. "Perfect," I thought, "I get to meet nine new people. The conversation should be lively." I was sadly mistaken. I quickly learned that all nine of my table mates were from the same organization on the East Coast. I also learned that their goal was to talk to each other as they excluded me from all conversation. When I tried to talk with the person next to me, the others would quickly draw his attention away from me. It was a most unrewarding experience for me.

In all honesty, it was unrewarding for their boss too. If I were their boss and had paid their travel and conference registration expenses, I would have been livid. I didn't need to spend thousands of dollars to have them eat together. I could have sent them to McDonald's or the company cafeteria and achieved the same result. They did nothing to enhance the reputation of their organization, which you would think nine people could do pretty well. They wasted my time and their boss's money.

So please, take advantage of the opportunity presented to you at large events and mingle. When you follow this advice, everyone benefits.

Okay, let's briefly recap this chapter. Assuming you are the guest at a business meal (meaning someone else or some group or organization invited you), you follow the leader right from the start. You arrive early and then wait for the leader to arrive. You move to the table only when invited to do so by the leader or his representative. You defer to the leader in terms of seat selection. You take your seat after the leader invites you to do so.

Once you have taken your seat, you follow the leader one more time before the meal service begins. At this stage of the meal, you earnestly apply the second guiding principle which is to remember that it **is about the relationship, the conversation, the business; it is not about the food or beverage**. You demonstrate this focus by removing your napkin after the leader.

This practice has waned a bit over the years, yet I still recommend it because it confirms that your focus is on the business, not the food. My grandmother explained it to me best. She said:

"Robert, as you know, your grandfather runs a success- ful business. Often he will invite potential clients or other business associates to our home for a meal. Despite this seemingly social environment, I understand that these are business meals. We hire a server and cook for the event, essentially catering the meal in our home.

The evening typically starts with cocktails which they enjoy in the den. When dinner is ready, I invite the group into the dining room. Prior to doing this and while escorting your grandfather and his guest(s) to the table, I listen in on their conversation.

Usually, they are engaged in small talk. You know: their golf game, the stock market, entertainment news, the weather, and so on. Boring stuff to me, but exciting to them. When I hear this, I lead them to the table, orchestrate the seating, and take my seat. They follow my lead. Once everyone has taken his or her seat, I remove my napkin and place it in my lap. This action is a signal to the server. It says that you may approach the table now and please start serving dinner.

However, sometimes I hear a conversation related to the business-at-hand. Maybe they are discussing terms of a contract or the advantages of working together. Whatever it is, I know it is important. They usually talk about such things later in the meal, most often after the staff has served the entrée and when interruptions are infrequent. But sometimes they get to it early, even before the meal begins.

When they do, I do NOT remove my napkin after I take my seat. I purposefully keep it on the table because this action is also a signal to the server. It tells him not to approach the table now and do not start serving dinner because an important conversation is taking place."

This wisdom convinced me that it is still a good idea to follow the leader when first removing your napkin from the table. Wait until he does it. When he removes his napkin, he is saying, *"Let's get to the meal."* When he does not remove his napkin, he may be saying, *"Before we think about eating, I'd like to talk about something important with you."*

When you leave your napkin on the table too, you send a reply that says, *"I am focused on this conversation too."* If you remove it before him, you risk sending a reply that says, *"I am not interested in your conversation and meaningless talk; I am here to eat."* You may as well tuck the napkin in your collar, grab your knife and fork, and pound them on the table while chanting, *"Grub, grub, give me grub!"*

Remove your napkin only after the leader confirms the agenda. When the leader's first topic is food, the napkin is removed from the table. When the leader prefers to start with conversation, the napkin remains on the table. Once the napkin is removed, it is time to place and use it correctly.

Chapter 7

How to Place and Use the Napkin

Most often, a linen napkin will be pre-set at your place setting. The most common folds are the triangle and the rectangular shapes. You should locate it easily; it looks like a napkin. You may have to search a little as sometimes the fold is a swan, crown, or some other nifty shape. The best place to look first is in front of you, in the center of your place setting. If it is not there, try looking to your left or right, slightly offset from your place setting. If that fails, try looking in your glassware, tucked away in a goblet.

The easiest way to find your napkin (and it really isn't as hard as I'm making it seem) is to follow the leader once again. After all, you will be watching the leader to see when she removes it. When she does, mirror her move as your place setting will be identical to hers. At a large event, when seated at a table far removed from the head table, wait until everyone sits and settles in before removing your napkin.

To remove your napkin from the table, use one hand to bring it to an area above your lap and slightly below the lip or edge of the table. This is where you will prepare it for your lap. Avoid doing so above your place setting and/or above the edge of the table. You are not a matador, so there is no need to wave it like a cape. Snapping is not necessary either.

Arranging the napkin for your lap slightly below the edge

of the table prevents embarrassment to you and your host if something falls out of the napkin. While this is rare, it is not out of the realm of possibilities. No matter how hygienic the kitchen, a crumb, piece of food, or hair can end up in a folded napkin.

Once you have the napkin positioned, use both hands to prepare it for your lap. We do not completely unfold a large linen napkin as we might a small one. Instead, we keep it folded in half. An unfolded, large napkin is likely to slip off your lap and onto the floor, especially when you consider the silkier, frictionless fabrics we wear at such meals. It's best to avoid dropping your napkin. Some say you may pick up a napkin that has fallen to the floor if you do so discretely, but I disagree. Picking a napkin off the floor and using it might cause people to question your hygiene practices. Simply ask the server for another napkin when this happens.

Depending on the complexity (or creativity) of the fold, we essentially rearrange a large napkin so we end up with a single half-fold. Then we place it in our lap with the fold facing us. *"Does it really matter where the fold is in your lap?"* you might ask. Yes, it does matter because the napkin should remain folded when you use it.

To use the napkin, you grasp a corner where the fold is and lift it to your lips. Then with that corner, you lightly blot or dab at your lips. Avoid aggressively scrubbing or wiping your face. Hand wiping and fingertip dabbing should be done below the table edge line. When a major cleansing is needed, excuse yourself and do so privately in the restroom.

The practice of dabbing at or blotting the lips started long ago, when travel was more challenging than today. A trip completed in a few hours today once took days, weeks, even months. As a result, extended visits were the norm. Upon arrival at your destination, you would often stay for days, if not weeks, at a time. This meant you would attend numerous dinners, often at the home of your host. Consequently, a courteous guest re-used his or her napkin for multiple meals, thereby reducing the expense for your host. A re-used napkin does not have to be cleaned and/ or replaced; a soiled napkin does. Ergo, one would blot or dab at their lips which kept the napkin relatively clean and serviceable for the next meal.

The reason why you place the fold closest to you, and why you grasp a corner with a fold when using the napkin, is equally practical. I mean, it's not as though people will be inspecting your lap to see how it is placed. At least I hope this is true. After all, gazing into another's lap might suggest your focus is not on business!

The rationale is simple—to avoid embarrassment when using the napkin. Imagine this scenario. You have just enjoyed a bite or two of your dinner roll. As a result, a few crumbs have fallen onto your lap. They are nestled on your napkin, unbeknownst even to you. You take a sip of water and reach for your napkin to blot the moisture from your lips.

When you grasp a corner with a fold as you should, the napkin will easily move to your lips with the fold intact. En route, the crumbs will

---

Napkin Necessities

1. Place your napkin in your lap after the leader places his. Rearrange the napkin and fold it in half, placing it in your lap with the fold closest to you.

2. To use the napkin, grasp a folded corner and lift to your lips. Blot while using; do not scrub.

3. When excusing yourself from the table (with the intent of returning), crumple your napkin and place it on the seat of your chair, or drape it over the back of your chair.

---

gently cascade off your napkin and into your lap. No one will be the wiser and you can casually brush the crumbs off your clothing, unnoticed by other guests.

However, if you grasp an unfolded corner and lift it to your lips, chaos may ensue. You might end up grasping only one of the two linen layers folded together. As you lift the napkin, the other layer may separate, causing the napkin to unfold completely. As it does, the crumbs may become projectiles, launched by the unfolding linen. At best, they will litter your place setting. At worst, they will fly through space and land in another guest's drink.

To visualize the difference, take an 8 ½" by 11" piece of paper and fold it in half so it looks more like a square than a rectangle. Pick up a corner of the folded end (there are only two from which to choose) and note how the paper remains folded. Now pick one corner of the open end (where there are four corners from which to choose) and see how the paper unfolds once again. It's the same principle but only with linen.

The napkin stays in our lap until the end of the meal unless we use it or have to leave the table during the meal. We will cover what to do when this happens (Chapter 16: Excuse Me: Cell Phones and Restrooms) and at the end of the meal (Chapter 21: Departing with Dignity) as we move through the meal. For now, the napkin is in our lap so it is time to discuss what we do next.

Chapter 8

Ordering: Moderation Matters

Continue to follow (or be) the leader even after you have arrived at the table, taken your seat, and placed your napkin in your lap. When dining at a restaurant, reviewing and ordering from the menu often comes next. At larger events, you or your host will often pre-select the menu for you, so you would omit this step.

When dining at a restaurant, a good leader or host will provide direction for the guest by saying something like, *"The chicken parmesan is very good here."* If you are the guest and you like chicken parmesan, this would be a good item to order. If you do not like chicken parmesan, you now know what price range you should choose. You also know the service style (plated entrée) and portion size to order. This holds true when the leader orders first. Again, you try to follow her lead. As mentioned earlier, not all leaders lead well so you may need to order your meal before the leader. Review the menu well to prepare for this situation, remembering **it is about the relationship, the conversation, the business; it is not the about the food or beverage**.

Start by reviewing the menu for price. Try to make a selection from the median range of prices. You need not order the least expensive item, nor should you order the most expensive. Order only one course. If she suggests and orders appetizers or dessert, you may follow her lead. Treat her expense account as if it were your precious childhood piggy bank, not as an open vault.

Then review the menu for content. Select items that are familiar to you and that are easy to eat. This is not the time to experiment with new menu items or with a new style of eating. Avoid messy foods too— large hamburgers, chicken on the bone, spaghetti (unless you are a skilled pasta spoon spinner), and so on. Generally, anything that squirts, slides, drips, or flips is not a good idea. Personally, I like to order a boneless chicken breast or a grilled portabella mushroom, as both can be easily eaten with a knife and fork.

If you have questions about an item, ask the server. It is also permissible to ask the server or the leader for suggestions. However, if you ask for a suggestion, treat it as a recommendation and follow it, especially when the leader provides it. To do otherwise **may** suggest you do not take advice well. Remember, being open to the wisdom of others, especially superiors and/or experts, is a desired quality to possess.

Before settling on your order, consider the portion size. Think of it as a test of your resource management skills. If you order too much or too little food, it **may** suggest that your budget management skills are lacking. Remember it's not about the food.

May is the key word here and worth exploring a bit. Etiquette is a subtle asset. I found that its impact is a lot like proper spelling and grammar. I learned this lesson a few years back.

My first task, as the newly named Director of University Auxiliary Services, was to submit a report to the Board of Directors recommending actions needed to improve student satisfaction with our bookstore and dining services operations. I completed the report and sent it to the 12 members of the board. The ideas, I believed, were brilliant.

The next day a friend of mine on the Board returned his copy to me. On it he had attached a post-it note that read, *"Please edit the mistakes as noted."* I looked over the report and saw that he had marked six or seven misspellings and/ or grammatical errors in red pen. This did not surprise me as I openly admit these are weaknesses of mine. I called to thank him for pointing the errors out, feeling slightly embarrassed that I hadn't proof read it more thoroughly. The phone call went like this.

"Thank you for pointing out my misspellings. I always struggle with that," I said. *"I'll take care of those right away."*

"Good," he replied.

"While I have you on the phone," I continued, *"can I ask you a question?"*

"Sure," he said. As you can tell, he was man of few words.

"What did you think of my ideas?" I asked. As I said, I was confident that they would improve student satisfaction immediately and significantly.

"To tell you the truth," he explained, *"I didn't notice the content; the errors were too distracting".*

This reply surprised me. I quickly sent out a revised copy of the report. When the Board finally met, the ideas were accepted and, once implemented, succeeded. As the meeting ended, I informally polled the rest of the Board about their reaction to the errors.

I learned that two other members (25% of the board) had the same reaction as my friend; they did not retain the content because the errors proved to be too distracting.

Three other members did not even notice the errors and thought the content was great. I would have shared their reaction. The rest of the Board (50%) noticed some of the errors, but not to the point where they missed the content. They too thought the ideas were good.

I have found that etiquette awareness often mirrors these findings. Inappropriate behavior will distract around 25% of those with whom you dine. About 50% of those with whom you dine might become distracted, but only if the errors become too egregious. Inappropriate behavior will not faze the final 25% because they do not know or care about etiquette. This is why I use the term **may** and why I say that etiquette is a subtle, yet powerful, skill. Why risk offending up to 25% of the people you work with, work for, or who work with you?

A simple concept to follow while ordering is that **moderation matters**. Be moderate in terms of price, in terms of portion, and in terms of pace—meaning you should keep pace with the table while eating. If you are the first one done eating, you may have focused too much on the food. If you are the last one eating, you may have done too much talking. I suggest you pause after every few bites, rest your flatware (Chapter 15: Knife and Fork Finesse), and check your pace. Then converse or eat as needed.

Many people have allergy concerns, special diets, or lifestyle choices that dictate what they can and cannot order. The best way to handle this situation is to call ahead when you can. Talk directly to the food service establishment, ideally a day ahead of time if possible. Just explain that you will be dining there the next day and have a specific dietary need. Then ask them what they suggest you order. Just something like, *"Hello, I will be having lunch at your restaurant tomorrow and am lactose intolerant. Can you recommend a dish or two that I might order?"* This not only lets you know what your options are, it lets them prepare something for you if necessary. This is particularly helpful at large, catered events with pre-set menus.

I worked for years in the hospitality industry and can tell you that chefs will work very hard to make sure your special need is met with a dish that is equal, if not superior, to those dishes being served to others. They will often special order items to meet your needs. This only works if they know about your need in advance.

The worse case scenario for you and for the kitchen is to wait until the last minute. Asking for a special item when you are ordering, or while they serve a catered meal, leaves the kitchen with limited options. Try to avoid this. If you haven't been able to call ahead, talk with a member of the staff as soon as possible. Arrive a little early and discretely ask to speak with the manager or chef. This gives them some time to prepare an alternative item.

Once you've ordered, the food will begin to arrive. Follow the leader when eating too; meaning the leader takes the first bite. Sometimes the leader may encourage you to start before they do. You may do so if everyone is served at the table and if two or three others are ready to start too. Avoid eating alone. Personally, I adhere to the "it's not about the food" guideline in this situation and wait for all to be served, even when encouraged to begin.

At a large event, wait until they serve everyone at your table before you begin. If served an item that not everyone has ordered (soup for example), ask the remaining table-mates if you can begin once you're sure that all who ordered the item have also been served. When you are the person not served, whether by choice or omission, encourage others to begin. The latter situation—omission—is a little tricky.

Sometimes, especially at large events, the wait staff will miss a guest while serving a course. As mentioned, I worked in the food biz for years, and can tell you that serving 1000 guests in 15 minutes is a monumental task. You start at one end of the room and move your way to the other. Wait staff use huge racks to bring out the food. When the racks are empty, a plate or two might be missing from a table. Ideally, that place is served first when a replenished rack appears, but sometimes servers forget. When this happens, simply encourage others to begin, excuse yourself from the table, and go speak—politely—to a server. If you want to avoid embarrassing others, you can exit the room after speaking with the server to make it appear as if you are going to the restroom. Avoid complaining, flagging down a server, or otherwise drawing attention to the oversight. Again, this may prove embarrassing to the leader.

A final note regarding those wonderful guiding principles is that you have a failsafe action: when in doubt, **follow the leader**. When you are unsure about when to eat or how to behave, wait until others eat or act, then follow their lead. The worst case scenario is that you will be making the same mistake they are which is better than doing it solo. An added benefit is that you can speak to others at the table while you wait, demonstrating your mastery of the second guiding principle: **it is about the conversation, the relationship, the business; it is not about the food or beverage**.

Chapter 9

Negotiating the Table: Utensils and Glassware

Of all the topics discussed in this book, the place setting causes the most consternation. People ask, *"What is that fork doing above my place setting?"* Others wonder, *"How do I handle the fish knife?"* I say don't sweat it because negotiating the table is not as complicated as it appears. I admit it can appear convoluted—just look at the list of potential utensils, plates, and glassware found on this page.

This is a relatively formal setting which some may never see. There are more formal settings than this, although the likelihood you will see one is rare. Still, settings like this can be intimidating. There are four forks, two spoons, two knives and a butter spreader. Throw in three

Formal Table Setting
(List of potential items)
1. Napkin
2. Fish Fork
3. Dinner or Main Course Fork
4. Salad Fork
5. Soup Bowl & Plate
6. Dinner Plate
7. Dinner Knife
8. Fish Knife
9. Soup Spoon
10. Bread & Butter Plate
11. Butter Spreader
12. Dessert Spoon and Fork
13. Water Goblet
14. Red Wine Goblet
15. White Wine Goblet

Negotiating the Table
- Left = 4 letters = fork & food (B & B plate).
- Right = 5 letters = spoon, knife, & glass.
- Create a small 'b' and 'd' with your index finger and thumb.
- Think BMW – bread, meat and water.
- Use utensils out-to-in.
- Use glassware as poured, from table edge to table center.

goblets, one bread and butter plate, and a napkin and we have 15 items. And this setting doesn't include a tea spoon which may be presented when served. Lions and tigers and bears, oh my—it's no wonder Dorothy is freaking out.

The good news is most place settings aren't this complicated. Often you will find two forks (salad and entrée), one spoon (tea or soup), one knife, and one or two pieces of glassware. The best news is, regardless of how many items you need to negotiate, you can do so with relative ease.

First, determine which bread and butter plate is yours, as well as which set of goblets or glassware you should use. Your bread and butter plate will usually be on your left and your drinks will be on your right. Think of it this way. The words left, fork, and food (as in bread and butter or food plate) all have four letters; all these items are on your left. The words right, spoon, knife, and glass all have five letters; all these items are on your right.

If this seems like too much work, make a little circle in each hand with fingers and your thumb as if you are making binoculars with your hands. Then extend your index finger. I caution you to do this under the table line in your lap so others won't see you doing this. Please resist the temptation to look through the binoculars—and you will be tempted! Look down and you will see that your left hand makes the letter "b" (for bread and butter plate) while your right hand forms the letter "d" (for drinks).

A final technique is to envision the meal going well, meaning you can buy the BMW you've always wanted. Envision those letters (not the car—this doesn't work so well then) on the table and follow them left-to-right. The "B" stands for bread and butter, the "M" for meal or meat, and the "W" for water. Pick the technique that works best for you.

Once the meal service begins, you use your utensils out-to-in. When a fork course is served, use the fork set to the far left. When you need a knife, use the one set to the far right. The service staff will clear the used utensil(s) after each course, so when the next fork course arrives, use the remaining fork set to the far left. When you need a knife again, use the remaining knife to the far right, and so on.

If you are still not sure what to use, simply engage in conversation and wait for others to start, and then follow their lead. This strategy also works when you don't know how to use a utensil, like a fish knife. Converse, observe, and then follow. It's a perfect solution!

You may find a pre-set plate centered between your utensils. This may be a service (also called cover or place) plate. This type of plate has a decorative function, serving as a visual center to the place setting. When used in this manner, we do not place food upon a service plate.

A final area to negotiate involves the glassware. This too is easier than you might think. Typically servers fill wine glasses only when used. The white wine goblet is often set closest to the table edge, indicating that it will be the first wine glass used with the fish course. The red wine goblet might be set behind it, ready for use with the entrée. The water glass will sit furthest from the table edge for use throughout the meal. Glassware will often be set sequentially, with the first glass used set closest to the table edge and ergo easiest to clear when the beverage is finished. An exception to this rule is a champagne flute that could be set to the right of the water glass, often for use during a toast.

You might already know that a true white wine goblet or champagne flute is long-stemmed, often with a relatively narrow bowl. Conversely, a red wine goblet or brandy snifter has a shorter stem and broader, deeper bowl. Each design has a functional purpose.

The long-stemmed glasses are for chilled beverages; wines and champagnes in particular. You hold this type of glassware by the stem so that your hand does not touch the bowl of the glass where the beverage is contained. When you do hold such glassware by the bowl, your body temperature transfers from your fingers or palm and will increase the temperature of the beverage, deteriorating the beverage's quality. Wine connoisseurs will note this faux pas as may others. When you hold chilled beverages by the bowl, condensation (moisture created when the chilled beverage warms) will make your hands clammy. So hold this type of glassware by the stem.

On the other hand, red wine (brandy too) is served at room temperature so your body temperature, again transferred from your fingers or palm, maintains the quality of the beverage. Consequently, you hold a red wine goblet and brandy snifter by the bowl, not by the stem.

Okay, you are at the table, comfortably seated with the napkin in your lap, and ready to negotiate the place setting. Now it really is time to eat.

SECTION THREE:

Let the Dining Begin: Soup, Salad, Bread, & Rolls

Chapter 10

Soup and Salad Made Simple

Finally we get to eat. Of course, we don't let the preliminaries bother us since we remember that it is about the relationship, the conversation, the business; it is not about the food and beverage. I should point out that this does not mean we ignore the food, nor does it mean that we resist complimenting or commenting positively about the dining experience. The leader has selected the location and often the menu so it is wise to confirm his good decision. Complimenting the food is perfectly acceptable, even advised. Conversely, speaking poorly of the food, the service, or the location is discouraged. There is no need to confirm someone's bad decision.

Soup will often be the first course served. Usually it is a hot soup as opposed to the less frequently served chilled soup or consommé. People often wonder how to best cool a too hot soup. Should they put an ice cube in it? Should they blow on it? Neither is correct. The quick answer is to let it cool naturally. You can accomplish this by adhering to the second guiding principle which is to remember that **it is about the relationship, the conversation, the business; it is not about the food or beverage**. The best way to let it cool naturally is to engage in conversation and build relationships. Blowing on it or putting ice in it communicates clearly that you are all about the food.

Once the soup is at an acceptable temperature and the leader has initiated consumption, you eat. The proper utensil for this course is the soup spoon which should be set to the far right. The bowl of the spoon is circular whereas most other spoon bowls have an oval shape. Take the soup spoon in your preferred hand (left is fine if you are left handed) and hold the spoon. Avoid gripping or tightly grabbing utensils. Instead, hold it somewhat loosely, almost as you would a pen or pencil. Try to hold it horizontally, balanced between the first knuckle of your middle finger and the tip of your index finger. Use your thumb to steady the handle.

Use your soup spoon to scoop away from you, across the top of the broth or consommé. Fill the bowl of the spoon about 2/3 full of broth and goodies. Then bring the spoon to your lips, letting it travel over the soup itself en route. We scoop away so that we can bring the filled spoon back over the soup, allowing any drops to fall into the soup bowl. If we were to scoop towards us, the drops would fall on the table linens or our lap. An etiquette guideline is to keep the table linens unsoiled which this move helps accomplish. It also helps us avoid standing at the end of the meal, only to find a nice soup stain in our lap!

Always bring the utensil to your lips, maintaining your posture. You may lean in a little (stiff backs are not required), ideally so that your chin line is over the edge line of the table. When you lean over your plate or over the table too

> **Soup and Salad Simplicity**
>
> **Soup**
> - Converse to Cool.
> - Scoop Away.
> - Sip, Don't Slurp.
> - Crackers = Crumbs.
>
> **Salad**
> - Use the salad fork to cut the salad; unless presented with a salad knife or when an item is too big to cut with the fork.
> - Dress as you go.

much, you are engaged in "trough style" dining which may be suitable for pigs, but is less so for humans.

When the soup spoon reaches your lips, sip—don't slurp—the soup. I know some cultures consider it a compliment when you slurp soup, so please do it there. However, we tend to be more reserved in expressing our culinary pleasure. Also, avoid the "airplane" insertion of the spoon into your mouth. You are not a parent feeding an infant so a direct attack is unnecessary. The handle of the spoon should be extended to your right (or left if left-handed) with the bowl of the spoon touching your lips. Then tilt the spoon, sip the soup, and swallow the goodies. Avoid placing the entire bowl of the spoon in your mouth.

Although crackers are a common accompaniment to soup, we do not place them into the soup—not a whole cracker, not a crumbled cracker, and definitely not crackers crumbled in the wrapper, then poured into the soup. (Although I admit that the latter works best if you're eating alone!) The exception is oyster crackers which we do add to chowders, either New England or Manhattan style. We can consume crackers as a side, eaten essentially as a cracker. Personally I avoid them since they are "crumb machines" and it is not about the food.

I adhere to the guideline "it's not about the food" when it comes to finishing the soup too. Etiquette standards say it is acceptable to tilt the soup bowl away from you (just as you scoop away) to get the last few drops. You may do this; however, my suggestion is you focus on conversation instead.

Salt and pepper is another potential pitfall during the soup course. Never salt and pepper or otherwise season soup (or any food item) until you have tasted it. To season first, then taste, **may** suggest that you make decisions without full information. After all, you have decided the soup needs help even before tasting it.

When finished with your soup, you can leave the soup spoon in the bowl, especially if the bowl is not set upon an under liner or saucer. If either of these is used, you can set it there instead with the handle facing out to the right.

Finally, remember to converse when not sipping. Take a sip or two, blot your lips with your napkin, and converse. That's why you are there!

When service is American style, the salad course follows the soup and precedes the entrée. When service is French style, the salad course follows the entrée. As mentioned earlier, the way your utensils are set will reveal the order of service. (See Chapter 9: Negotiating the Table: Utensils and Glassware.) Either way, you will use the fork set to your far left for the salad course. You can often distinguish it from the entrée fork because it has shorter tines and a thicker base.

The salad fork has a dual purpose—to cut as well as to pierce. The entrée fork has a single purpose—to pierce. Ergo, they differ in design. You will still find some salad forks that have a knife-like edge on the left tine. This is because in many countries one does not use the knife to cut the salad unless presented with a salad knife. This was true in the United States too until the 1980s or so.

Consequently, it is still a good idea to do your cutting with the salad fork unless presented with a salad knife. When only one knife is set on the table, it is most likely not a salad knife; it is an entrée knife. Now you might think to yourself, *"Self, what if I want to cut into a nice, juicy looking cherry tomato? Is Mr. Shutt suggesting that I grab my salad fork, lean into it, and risk spraying myself or my neighbors with tomato juice? Doesn't he realize that I might also propel the halved tomato onto the table?"* No, I am not saying that.

Use of the entrée knife with the salad is usually an acceptable move, especially if you are cutting a particularly large item (cherry tomato, cucumber slice, etc). However, when you do use a knife, remember that used utensils do not touch the table linens. You must rest the knife horizontally, with the serrated or sharp edge facing towards you, on your salad plate.

A more important point related to the cherry tomato question is this: do you really need to invest so much thought and effort into a cherry tomato? Were it I, I would remember that it is about the conversation, not the food. Consequently, I would feel perfectly comfortable leaving the cherry tomato alone so that I could focus on the conversation.

The fact that this guideline evolved over time is significant primarily because it is important to know that guidelines can change. This is yet another reason why it is so important to **follow the leader**. Following the leader helps you keep current with change. Change is rare, but it does happen as this guideline proves.

As to why it changed, my guess is that it was a result of American eating habits. It is no surprise that we love large portions. This passion is not limited to fast food. It manifests itself in almost every facet of dining, including salads. Our love for big, chunky salads has made use of the knife with salad more of a necessity than a luxury.

Salads are often served pre-dressed, meaning they apply the dressing in the kitchen. When served a salad dressed in this manner, feel free to disperse the dressing by lightly tossing or mixing the salad, ideally using only your salad fork. This move is also acceptable when the dressing is pre-set in a bowl or salad boat that everyone at the table shares. When served in this manner, use the common spoon provided to dollop dressing onto your salad and replace this spoon when finished so the next guest can use it. Then use your salad fork to disperse and lightly toss the salad.

Having your individual salad dressing served on the side is a third style of service. When served in this manner, you may elect to "dress as you go", especially at a formal event. You pour a little over the top of the salad and eat that portion of the salad without tossing. Then you add a little more and eat the next level, again without tossing.

When finished with the salad, leave your fork on the salad plate with the handle extending horizontally out to the right. Image a clock face: center the tines in the middle of the plate with the fork handle sitting at two o'clock. If you've used a knife too, place the knife above the fork with the sharp edge facing towards you. More detail about knife and fork placement will be provided later in Chapter 15: Knife and Fork Finesse.

Chapter 11

Fancy Passing:
Dinner Rolls, Bread, and Butter

It is common to see bread products like dinner rolls served with the soup or salad course. They can also be pre-set prior to the arrival of guests. Either way, they are often the first item passed from one guest to another which means this is a good time to discuss the rules of passing. Although these rules apply to almost any item passed, our primary focus will be on dinner rolls. Just use these guidelines for any other passed item: creamers, sugars, pre-set salad dressing, etc.

For the moment, let's assume dinner rolls are served in a basket. The first rule of passing is that when it is time for the item to be passed, whoever is closest to the item initiates passing whether they intend to enjoy the item or not. Remember the leader initiates dining, so don't be overly eager to pass the rolls. Wait until another course has been started or for an invitation from the leader.

The second rule is that the person who initiates the passing does not take the item. Instead, they wait until it moves around the table before taking any; courtesy dictates this move. The passer wants to be sure that everyone else is served first. Some restaurants purposefully serve one less dinner roll than the number of guests of the table.

The third rule is to pass to the right when passing for the

first time. The rationale for this action is simple: it reduces the likelihood of an accident. Most people are right-handed so they drink, and often eat, with their right hand. When we pass to the right, we are essentially serving from the left, just as servers have done for years (serve to the left, clear from the right).

Go ahead and envision this with your hands. Imagine you are talking to someone to your left as you pass a basket of dinner rolls with your right hand to the person seated to your right. The basket enters her personal space from the left. So even if she does not know the basket is arriving, the chance of an accident is minimal. If she's taking a drink, it's probably with her right hand. If she's taking a sip of soup or a bite of salad, it too is probably with her right hand. The worse that can happen is that you will nudge her left elbow a bit.

Imagine you are talking to someone on your right and you pass to the left. Now the basket arrives from the right. If no one is paying attention, there is a chance you will nudge his elbow while he takes a sip of soup or a bite of salad. Bam! You spill soup or salad onto the table or into his lap. Worse yet, he could be taking a drink. You nudge his elbow and you spill red wine on his shirt or you chip his tooth. All the above are avoidable accidents when you initiate passing to the right.

There are some exceptions to these rules. One relates to dinner rolls. The initiator can make an optional, courtesy-based move before passing to the right. Assume that you are closest to a basket of dinner rolls and initiate the passing. Instead of passing immediately to the right, you present the basket to the person to your left, keeping hold of the basket as you do so. If a cloth covers the rolls, open the cloth so he has access to the rolls and say, *"Would you care for a dinner roll?"* He may take one or decline your offer. When either occurs, you re-cover the rolls with the cloth and then pass the basket to your right. Remember you do not take any at this time.

The person on your right to whom you have just passed the basket of dinner rolls will then do one of two things. One action could be he simply takes a dinner roll and passes the basket to his right. When this happens, you—the initiator—wait until the basket makes its way around the table before selecting a roll of your own.

The other action could be an offering to you, meaning he keeps hold of the basket and offers a roll to you because you are seated to his left. When this occurs, you may select a dinner roll. Whenever anyone offers you dinner rolls, or any other passed item in this manner, you may accept the offer. This is true even when you have initiated the passing. However, if no one offers them to you, do not take one until they have made their way around the table. The initial offering to the left, while keeping hold of the passed service container,

---

Bread & Butter Basics / Fancy Passing

Bread and Butter

- Place dinner roll on your bread and butter (B & B) plate.
- Place butter on your B & B plate.
- Tear, rip, or break a piece of roll. Do not use a knife to cut.
- Tear, rip, or break over your B & B plate.
- Spread butter on the torn piece with your butter spreader or dinner knife.
- Rest the used butter spreader or knife on your B & B plate.

Fancy Passing

- When an item is passed, the person closest to the item initiates the passing.
- The person who initiates the passing does not take any of the items.
- When initiating passing, pass to the right. When passing upon request, take the shortest route.
- Do not hand-off salt and pepper, table-pass instead.
- Pass salt and pepper together.

works well with some other items too, most notably butter pats and pre-set salad dressing.

When offered a dinner roll or other bread item, place it on your bread and butter (B & B) plate when one is provided. Do the same thing with butter; place a pat or small amount on your B & B plate. If there is no B & B plate, place it on your service plate or dinner plate. Better yet, if there is no B & B plate, go ahead and take a pass on the rolls. After all, it's not about the food; it's about the business.

Then you tear, break, or rip a piece of bread or roll to either eat or to spread butter on it. Do this above the B & B plate instead of directly in front of you so crumbs will fall on the plate, not your lap or your place setting. We do not use a knife to cut the bread or roll. In fact, the name of the knife-looking utensil that might be on your B & B plate is a butter spreader, revealing its intended purpose. Once you've removed a piece, you may go ahead and eat it. If you choose to spread butter on it, use your butter spreader or dinner knife (if no spreader is provided) to place some of the butter from your B & B plate onto your roll or bread.

Used utensils do not touch the table linens, so rest the utensil used for spreading on your B & B plate horizontally with the cutting edge facing towards you. Used utensils never touch the table linens because they could soil the linens. Not only is this the same principle that guides napkin use (Chapter 7: How to Place and Use the Napkin), it may also leave you dining from a messy place setting.

Finally, never take the last dinner roll, or any other communal item, set on the table. Ideally, you should let the leader decide to replenish. At a large event with no discern-able leader, replenish when one or two rolls are left; human nature dictates this. It's like watching someone yawn. If you see them do it a time or two, you will yawn yourself.

Likewise, when others see you take another dinner roll, they often decide they want one too. Don't leave them with none; replenish for all before you personally restock.

A final tip involves the passing of salt and pepper shakers. As mentioned earlier, we never season before tasting (Chapter 10: Soup and Salad Made Simple). As a result, we do not initiate the passing of the salt and pepper; we pass only when requested by another. We also pass both the salt and the pepper together, even when asked for only one or the other. Since we pass only when requested, we select the shortest path to the requester even if it means passing to the left. If someone along the passing route wants some too, he should wait until after the requester has used them.

Finally, we do not hand-off the salt and pepper shakers. We place them on the table within reach of our requester who picks them up by the base and places them on the table for the next user, and so on. This ensures that we handle only the base of the shakers, not the caps where the seasoning exits. If we hand-off the shakers, the passer would hold the shakers by their base and leave the receiver only the cap to grasp. This means that the hand touches the cap which is a hygiene concern. We just don't know how clean the hands of others are so it's best to avoid touching food service surfaces.

For now, congratulate yourself as it's almost time for the main event—the entrée! Actually, that's a bit of a test since you know by now that it's about the conversation, etc.; it's not about the food or beverage. So while we want to appreciate the quality of the food, our focus is on the people with us. It's also a bit of tease too, since the entrée is still three chapters away.

Chapter 12

Surprise: Sorbets and Fingerbowls

Sorbet is a somewhat uncommon yet acceptable course still served today. The more formal the dinner, the more likely it is that you will be served sorbet. Sorbet is a fruit flavored dish that looks an awful lot like sherbet or ice cream. Do not be fooled. Sorbet is not dessert and it is not an actual course; it is a palate cleanser. When served a sherbet-like item mid-meal, assume it is sorbet.

Sorbet typically precedes the entrée. The function of this palate cleanser is to eliminate the lingering after-taste of the previous course so that you can fully appreciate the culinary sensations yet to come. Therefore, you take as many bites as you need to achieve this goal. One or two bites are fine, provided your palate is cleansed.

Another item that may appear after a seafood course is a fingerbowl. The purpose of the fingerbowl is to clean your fingertips which may have gotten a bit greasy after such a course. It may include a garnish such as a slice of lemon or a flower. Leave those in it.

To use the fingerbowl, gently dip your fingertips into the water and then dry them off delicately with the napkin provided for this purpose. When finished, set the bowl to the left side of your place setting, moving it (and any saucer or under liner served with it) with both hands.

Interestingly enough, a fingerbowl earned former

President John F. Kennedy entrance into the mythical etiquette hall-of-fame. I heard the story this way.

President Kennedy held a White House dinner to honor a visiting foreign dignitary. Seafood was the featured entree. As is New England custom, fingerbowls followed the seafood course. The foreign dignitary, unfamiliar with the fingerbowl and no doubt confused by the floral garnish, assumed it was a clear broth. Consequently, he picked up the bowl with both hands and drank from it, smiling broadly in appreciation. Silence filled the room as the crowd pondered how to react to this obvious faux pas.

President Kennedy did not want his guest to feel embarrassed, so he followed suit, picking up his fingerbowl and drinking from it too. The rest of the guests followed the leader and drank from their bowl as well.

Kennedy's example is an important illustrative story because Kennedy tactfully ensured that his guest was not embarrassed and demonstrated that we do not use our etiquette knowledge to correct others. Instead, we use it to ensure that we shine through, as Kennedy did.

Chapter 13

Business Versus Social Etiquette

Before we get to the entrée, there is an important topic to discuss. You might have been thinking about it already, wondering to yourself, *"Self, what is with the limited knife use during the early part of the meal? There is no cutting of the dinner roll? It's called a butter spreader when it looks like a knife. You are encouraged to cut the salad with your salad fork? What's the story?"* Well I'm glad you asked because the story and the reasoning behind it help to illustrate the difference between business and social etiquette.

I believe the most significant moment in the history of appropriate professional behavior occurred during medieval times, predating the use of the word *etiquette*. The word *etiquette* is of French origin, attributed to the court of King Louis XIV who ruled from 1643 to 1715. However, as Ptahhotep illustrates (Chapter 2: Why It Matters), many of the professional behavior guidelines we use today predate King Louis.

The idea of written rules of appropriate behavior flourished during the medieval era which occurred between the 12th and 15th centuries. The knight, or *chevalier*, was a central figure in this "age of chivalry". The knight served his lord—not Lord as in God above, but lord as in dude with lots of land and power. These medieval knights valued valor and honor.

During this time, authors like de Meun, Bonet, and Machiavelli wrote books extolling the "Rules of War" in an attempt to bring honor to warfare, as ironic as that may seem. They preached behaviors like *"thou shalt not recoil before thine enemy"* and *"thou shalt respect all weaknesses and shalt constitute thyself the defender or them"*. You know—typical office conduct. After all, a knight's profession was warfare. You report for work at an office or retail outlet; they reported to work on the battlefield or in the castle. You say toe-mate-o; I say toe-ma-toe.

Now you might point out that regardless of how extreme our office environment is today, it is far removed from a medieval battlefield—true that. However, in some ways our work environment resembles another area of concern for a knight—the table of peace.

A main goal of warfare is cessation of hostilities. I am talking ideals here so bear with me. As much as the knight might enjoy heated battle in full body armor, the goal was to get the enemy to give up so the two sides could negotiate a peace treaty. They would hold meetings and share meals, working out the details of this contract just as we do in the world of work today. While negotiating terms of co-existence, they were essentially making a sale, agreeing to a contract, and closing the deal. Consequently, they developed "Rules of War" which addressed behavior in this business-type environment too. Many of the behaviors introduced then continue today.

Take the handshake for example. The handshake, in all its various forms, may be the most accepted business gesture in the world. In medieval times, feuding knights used it when they met to discuss terms of surrender—the terms of co-existence. Most people are right-handed, meaning the right-hand is the "weapon hand". So when a knight extended an empty right-hand to his enemy, it non-verbally communicated that he was not armed, that he came in peace.

The extended open-faced, weapon-free hand communicated the intended agenda. When met with another open-faced, weapon-free hand, they confirmed the agenda with a clasp. In medieval times, a mutual left-handed frisk accompanied this clasp, typically from shoulder to hips. This confirmed the meeting would be free of sabotage and could now begin. This greeting continues today but without the left-hand frisk.

Another gesture (still used today by the world's armies) signaled the transition from battle to business. Imagine you have traveled through time and find yourself watching the leader of a drove of knights. He is fatigued from a day of hand-to-hand warfare. His heavy armor creates substantial sweat. He struggles to breathe in his thick, chain-mail helmet. Both sides have lost men. Many more lie critically wounded. He decides to call an end to the battle. The knight remains fully armored as he approaches the rival leader. The threat of sabotage, even assassination, is high. Only when he is toe-to-toe with his rival will they talk, not before. He takes his last step and plants his feet. Then and only then, the knight raises his right arm, free of weapons, and lifts the visor that shields his eyes during combat. The use of the right hand shows that the knight's fighting hand is unarmed. This gesture alone is a significant action. The knight is also displaying great trust in his rival by presenting to him a most vulnerable target— his brain. A well-placed dagger-through-the-eye can kill. This gesture or salute signifies he knows the time for fighting has passed. This salute indicates that the two sides now have an aligned intent. The agenda has changed. Both these gestures, the salute and the handshake, build an atmosphere of collaboration and cooperation, an atmosphere most conducive to business success.

As mentioned, the goal of warfare is peace. In medieval times, warring factions typically celebrated an agreement of peace with a feast. The leaders of one fiefdom invited the opposing leaders to their castle to celebrate. After checking their weapons at the door, the two parties would embark upon on long night of food and drink. When all went well, the evening ended with a strong bond of allegiance. The problem was the evening could go wrong—very, very wrong.

Early on, some leaders (usually those with inferior forces) devised an alternative plan for conquest: specifically, sabotage!

Let's imagine that the Kingdom of Arthur has been at war with the Kingdom of Cole for decades. Neither side can deliver the final blow. One day, the leaders of the Kingdom of Arthur decide to end the madness. They feign surrender to the Kingdom of Cole, agree to terms, and invite all the leaders of the Kingdom of Cole to come celebrate the peace. The leaders of the Kingdom of Arthur gather the unarmed leaders of the Kingdom of Cole into the mead hall or banquet room and then they kill them. Assassination is the special of the day! The leaders of the Kingdom of Arthur then go back to the Kingdom of Cole and inform the people that all the leaders are dead and it is now a part of the Kingdom of Arthur.

This ruse worked quite well a time or two until hosts seeking a peaceful solution learned to create an environment that confirmed collaboration and cooperation by developing behaviors that discouraged violence. Let's look at some current dining habits that have their origins from this time period.

The first is the toast—not the bread slices you slap with butter or jam, but the tradition of raising a glass to welcome and honor others. This action most likely started before the medieval age; however, the methodology changed when sabotage became a concern. This concern led to the custom of clinking goblets.

Imagine again that we are in the Kingdoms of Arthur and Cole. I rule the Kingdom of Arthur and the Kingdom of Cole invites me to its castle to celebrate peace. Although I am suspicious of the intent, I accept the invitation. Once seated, the ruler of the Kingdom of Cole rises to greet my posse and me. He proposes a toast to me.

I raise my glass (actually, it was most likely a pewter or lead goblet as glassware wasn't being used then) and forcefully clink it against his. Specifically, I clink with enough force to be sure some of my beverage spills into his goblet. He then takes a drink from the goblet which has a blend of his beverage and mine. I then adhere to another toasting guideline that we follow today. I do not drink a toast to myself; instead, I nod in appreciation and watch him drink. I continue to watch him for a few minutes. If he remains standing and in good health, I proceed with the meal as I now know that he has not tried to poison me. However, if he has an altered demeanor or if he refuses to drink the toast, I know the agenda is assassination, not peace, and the battle begins.

Medieval hosts quickly learned about this ploy, aban-doned any attempts at mischief, and the toast became a symbolic start to a successful meal. The toast confirms that the focus is on a single agenda, peace (or at the very least non-aggression).

The custom of clearing used utensils after each course is another practice that evolved from this focus. At these early meals when warring factions genuinely met to celebrate peace, one could always change his mind. Maybe the meal was disappointing, or perhaps the jester was not particularly funny. Most likely, the consumption of mass quantities of grog and mead emboldened them. The connection between alcohol consumption and violence was known even then. Regardless, when the meal was winding down, a well-intended guest would occasionally decide that peace was not the path to follow. Once again, the hosts knew this and planned accordingly.

Guests often checked their weapons when they entered the banquet hall; that was one safeguard. Another was the clearing of the utensils after each course. At the beginning of the meal when everyone was relatively sober, the table was set with a plethora of utensils, primarily knives and spoons (or chips as they were called then). Forks came later, invented by members of France's high society. At the end of the meal when virtually no one was sober, the utensils, or potential weapons, were gone. The guests had no choice but to stick to the agenda of peace. Even if a fight did break out, it would turn into a brawl, not murder. Peace could survive a brawl.

Once introduced, forks quickly became popular. They looked more like a farm implement than a military weapon, so their usage clearly confirmed a non-aggressive agenda; hence, the current custom of limited knife use early in the meal. The fork is so relatively passive in appearance that many still use it to butter a baked potato, avoiding the knife yet again. When I fly to a speaking engagement, security confirms the perceived passivity of the pronged utensil of decorum (the fork). I routinely carry a set of utensils for demonstration purposes. Security always confiscates my dinner knife; they never confiscate my fork.

This is why I believe medieval times are when the foundation **focus on a single agenda** originated. These behaviors—the handshake, the salute, the toast, the clearing of utensils, and limited knife use—all confirm that the focus is cooperation, not assassination.

Another foundation covered in the "Rules of War" concerned the knight's relationship with his boss. A commonly used title for his boss was "lord" which reveals the depth of his commitment to service. A knight deferred to his lord's wishes. A knight accommodated his behavior to suit the needs of his superior. He did not enter the lord's chamber until invited to do so. He sat only after the lord did, or invited him to do so. When speaking, the lord had his complete attention. Knights knew it was important to be respectful of their employer since these actions demonstrated that the knight understood and respected the hierarchy, a hierarchy based on one's power within the fiefdom. As you know, this foundation—**respect the hierarchy**—remains a cornerstone of appropriate professional behavior today.

This foundation also represents an essential difference between social and business etiquette. Both adhere to the foundation "respect the hierarchy" since one's power within the environment dictates the hierarchy of both. However, power in the social world is more gender specific. A look at another set of medieval "rules" tells us why; these are the "Rules of Courtly Love".

When not engrossed in negotiations or doing battle, a knight often found himself pursuing the affection of a lady (which remains an appropriate social etiquette term).

Consequently, gender dictates social hierarchy, not organizational structure. This is the major difference between social and business etiquette.

At these times, a knight adhered to these "Rules of Courtly Love", not the "Rules of War", since his ability to display appropriate deference and accommodation authenticated his understanding of the social hierarchy. The knight wanted the approval of his woman of interest and many social etiquette customs reflect this reality.

"Ladies first" is a phrase heard even today. A gentleman still pulls out the chair and holds the door open for his lady. He may also walk closest to the curb. Today we do so in case a vehicle drives through a puddle and sprays water onto the sidewalk so that the man gets drenched, not the woman. A woman's cleanliness is of paramount importance, so a gentleman defers to this reality.

This practice got its start in Europe, again during medieval times. Vehicles were not the main concern—hygiene was. This was way before indoor plumbing. It was even before people determined the source of bacteria that polluted the public water supply. The practice then was to collect your toilet waste in bowls and toss it out your window. It would then literally flow down the center of the street in an open sewer to the nearest creek or river. This influenced the architectural design of the day as many homes had an overhung second floor. People would walk close to the building, away from the center of the street and under the overhang. The toilet water, when thrown from the second floor, would then miss them. However, occasionally the water would dribble down onto an unsuspecting pedestrian. To ensure that his lady remained unsoiled, a gentleman would walk on the outside, to insure that it was he that got drenched.

While it is important to note the difference between business and social etiquette, you should know the boundaries are hazy at best, especially when it comes to social niceties like chairs and doors. The Northeast United States recognizes the distinction more than most other regions. Gender is often not a factor in business etiquette, so men take a risk when they pull out chairs or open doors for women just because they are women. Similarly, women take a risk when they let men pull out chairs or open doors for them.

The risk for women is that they may send a message that says view me as a woman first and as a professional second. The risk for men is that they may send a message that says I view you as a woman first and as a professional second. This is not to say that I encourage women to boldly state that they can *"get their own chair"* when a man attempts such kindness. Instead, I suggest that women consider the motivation of the man extending such a kindness. If it is clear that he sees you as woman first and a peer or professional second, you might want to get to that chair or door ahead of him so you can get it yourself.

The professional guidelines are simple. Whoever gets to the door first opens the door for those who follow. I admit that I have a knack for getting to the door slightly ahead of potential clients and other situational superiors. Of course I don't elbow them out of way and race to the door; it's a bit more subtle than that. As for chairs, you help people with chairs only when they need help. Help might be required because someone is loaded with materials. Help might also be required because of a physical challenge.

I learned this lesson from my mother who was the first woman Executive Director of a traditionally male non-profit in one of our most populous states. Once she invited me to attend a chamber luncheon with her. On the way there, she gave me specific instructions.

"Robert," she said, "I am here as the Executive Director, not as a woman and not as your mother. So please do not pull out my chair or open the door for me unless you happen to get to the door first."

She explained that she wanted to be sure that everyone viewed her as a professional and a peer, not as a woman or a mom (which may be redundant).

Years later after she retired, this organization presented her with a lifetime achievement award. This was after she had won a battle against cancer, sacrificing a leg in the victory. Once again she invited me to join her. I did not need direction this time as I knew that I should help her with the door and with her chair. I helped not because she was a woman or my elder, but because she required my help.

This chapter should make it clear that medieval knights first practiced many business behaviors and social courtesies used today. They also knew the difference between a business and social situation. The fact that appropriate behavior has been valued for hundreds of years does not mean that etiquette is antiquated. Instead, it just means etiquette has withstood the test of time and should be respected and valued.

Chapter 14

Remember: Shine Through by Eliminating Distracting Behavior

Assuming you now understand the eternal value of appropriate behavior, you might not fully appreciate the subtle power it possesses. Earlier (Chapter 2: Why It Matters) I explained that I have interviewed hundreds of job applicants while explaining how important interpersonal communication skills are to your career success. Etiquette is an interpersonal communication skill, a skill that **lets you shine through**, sometimes in a most subtle manner.

Let's imagine I have an opening on my management team. I invite two final candidates to a dinner interview. Let's say their names are Jason and Jennifer. It's not as though I will walk away from the interviews and think to myself:

*"Let me see, Jason or Jennifer, Jason or Jennifer, who did I like best? It's hard to decide who was best. Well, I think I **will** offer the job to Jason because he really sipped his soup superbly. I have never seen such a super soup sipper. I want him to work with me. Jason gets the job because of his superb dining etiquette skills."*

That is a ludicrous scenario, as is thinking this:

"Let me see, Jason or Jennifer, Jason or Jennifer, who did I like best? It's hard to decide who was best. Well, I think I **will not** offer the job to Jason because he used his knife to cut his dinner roll. I cannot believe he was so uncouth. I thought he was field dressing an eight-point buck that he bagged during deer season. Jennifer gets the job because of Jason's lack of dining etiquette skills."

This is equally ludicrous as the impact is rarely so direct. What is more likely is this scenario:

I have prepared for these interviews. I have a list of identical questions that I will ask both Jason and Jennifer so that I maintain objectivity. I've already reviewed their experience and spoken with their references, so it is no longer a question of who can perform the job. This is all about who will best fit into my organization. Since I am a seasoned interviewer, I included one or two questions that are the real dealmakers (or deal-breakers). I will be most interested and attentive to those answers. The rest is fluff.

Jason did reasonably well in his interview; however, I am not overly impressed with his response to a key question. His response was adequate, yet not earth shaking. I hope for better with Jennifer. After they serve the soup, I ask this question. Unbeknownst to me, Jennifer has prepared for this question. She has researched and rehearsed her response. She knows that if I ask this question, she will rock the answer. Her moment has arrived.

She makes eye contact with me and pauses for a moment, as if reflecting upon her response. As she pauses, she casually—perhaps even absent-mindedly—picks up a packet of saltines served with the soup. She begins to respond. As *she does, she crumbles the crackers up in the cellophane wrapper to maximize the crumb quality and content. I can't help but notice this move. She continues to speak. As she does, she opens the cellophane and pours the crackers into her soup. She ends her response and then she stirs the crackers into the soup, creating a perfect mush in the process.*

I leave the interview and ponder the performance of both Jason and Jennifer. I remember that Jason's response to my key question was adequate. But what was Jennifer's response? I can't seem to recall what it was she said. All I remember is her crushing the crackers like a junk car at a salvage yard.

Jennifer's inappropriate actions distracted me from listening to her response. Although it was exactly what I hoped to hear, I missed it.

"Oh well", I conclude. "I guess I'll make the offer to Jason."

This illustrates the subtle power of appropriate behavior. It really is that simple—and that powerful.

SECTION FOUR:

The Main Event: The Entrée and So Much More

Chapter 15

Knife and Fork Finesse

The first thing to know about the "main event" (also known as entrée service) is that the most important conversations often occur during this part of the meal. Prior to entrée service, small talk predominates. The appearance of the entrée indicates that service staff interruptions will be minimal: no more explaining specials, taking orders, or serving and clearing of preliminary courses. This truly is the "main event" in terms of meal service and conversation. If business is on the agenda, the floor opens now. Ironically, it is also when multiple utensil use (both knife and fork) is most encouraged; therefore, they must be handled with finesse so that you can continue to focus on the business, not the food or beverage.

I will note that my focus will be on American style service, when the entrée follows the salad course. Service could be French style, meaning the salad follows the entrée. However, American style is most common in America (imagine that) so that is the flow I am following. Regardless and at long last, use of the knife is now fully embraced (Chapter 13: Business Versus Social Etiquette), so let's review how to use the knife and fork together.

You know by now that you will use the outermost remaining fork and the outermost (and often only) knife. You may need only the fork for the accompanying sides:

vegetables, potatoes, and such. However, for the entrée itself and some sides, you may also need the knife to cut, slice, or trim. There are two acceptable ways to use the knife and fork together, the American (or Zig Zag) style and the Continental style.

With both styles, you start with the knife in your dominant (or weapon) hand. Despite this, remember these utensils are not weapons, so do not grasp them tightly, hold them vertically, or wave them about dramatically. The sharp (or cutting) edge of the knife **always** faces towards you, not other diners. Your agenda is peace which these actions confirm. I am right-handed so I will describe the styles as if eating this way. If you are left-handed, simply reverse what I say.

When dining American style, the knife is in your right hand and the fork in your left. With the tines of the fork facing down, pierce and secure the item you wish to cut, slice, or trim. Note that the "tines" are the three or four extensions with points found on the end of the fork. Then with your right hand, use the knife to cut, slice, or trim. When cutting an entrée (such as a boneless chicken breast), make one or two cuts at a time. Be sure to let the knife do the cutting. Avoid leaning into the knife or sawing fero-ciously with it; that's a bit too much about the food. When confronted with such a challenge, I converse instead.

Once you've made the cut, rest your knife upon your dinner plate, ideally with the point at eleven o'clock and the handle at two o'clock (when you imagine the plate as a clock face) and with the cutting edge facing towards you. Once the knife is resting, you switch the fork from your left hand to your right hand with the tines now facing up. Then you go ahead and use the fork to secure and eat your food, bringing it to your mouth with the tines up. Be sure to bring the food to you rather than leaning down to bring yourself to the food.

When dining Continental style, start just as you did for the American style with the fork in your left hand (tines down) and the knife in your right. Make the cut and rest the knife as outlined above. This is where the similarities end. The fork now remains in your left hand and the tines also remain pointing down. You then use the fork to secure and eat your food, bringing it to your mouth with the tines down.

You may mix-and-match as often as you like. For example, I like to eat items I cut with the knife Continental style. I also like to eat side items that do not require a knife using the American style. I do so with full confidence and urge you to do so too. My only caveat is to keep the guideline "follow the leader" in mind. The American style is universally accepted in the United States (again, imagine that) whereas there are still pockets of resistance to the Continental style. For example, my grandmother was not fond of the Continental style. When I dined with her, I used only the American style.

Regardless of which method you use, remember to rest your knife along the top edge of the plate after making a cut. In some cultures, one holds the knife constantly while dining. To me, this move is a little too much about the food, so I like to rest the knife.

I suspect this habit of holding onto the knife at all times had medieval origins, especially since these cultures also discouraged resting your hands under the table while pausing or conversing. My guess is both behaviors served a purpose in the old medieval feasts. Holding onto your knife reduced the likelihood of a surprise attack. Keeping your hands visible reduced the likelihood of hidden daggers or the discrete mixing of poison under the table. Needless to say—and yet I will—when dining in such a culture, you should follow the leader.

Please keep in mind that no cultural habit is superior or inferior to another; all have evolved for logical reasons. As I said in the introduction, this book focuses upon specific North American guidelines. I respect all behavioral guidelines. When I write about the differences, I do so out of respect and for the purpose of education.

Finally, remember to cut only a piece or two at a time. Avoid cutting up the entire entrée as a parent might do for a toddler. Some say you should cut only when pulling the knife towards you, not while pushing it away from you. This way you reduce the likelihood of accidentally pushing a bit of food onto the center of the table, potentially soiling the cloth and drawing unwanted attention to yourself. I say this is optional, meaning it is your choice.

While enjoying your entrée, remember that moderation matters with regard to pace. Ideally, all diners at the table should start and finish each course at about the same time. I suggest that you monitor your progress during each course. Simply enjoy a bite or two and then rest your utensils, pause, and converse with someone. Take a quick glance at other diners' plates to see if you are on pace. If you are ahead of the pace and too much of your food is gone, talk for a while, ideally with someone else who is ahead of the pace. If you are behind the pace and not enough food is gone, shorten the conversation and take a few extra bites at a reasonable pace. Don't wolf it down to catch up; just talk a little less.

This is a good rule of thumb. If you are often the last one finished at the table, you might be doing too much talking. If you are often the first one finished, you might be doing too much eating. Either way, strive to find balance in your pace.

When you do pause to converse, you should rest your utensils. The question is: where and how do you rest them? This is an area of great debate. Well, not "great debate" as in the Lincoln-Douglas debates that preceded the Civil War. Not even "great debate" like the eternal Mac versus PC question. Yet in the world of dining etiquette, it is one of two areas where disagreement runs rampant.

Proponents support at least four or five different locations. This is true when it comes to the final position of rest too, signifying that you are finished and that your plate can be cleared. Fortunately while researching this topic, I found some areas of universal agreement which guide my recommendations.

For example, we all agree that the knife should remain to the right and/or above the fork. This mirrors their place setting positions: knife to the right, fork to the left. When using the Continental style, you rest your fork to the left with the handle at about eight o'clock and the tines centered on the plate. The knife is to the right with the handle at four o'clock and the tip centered on the plate. They form a ^. When using the American style, you rest your fork with the handle at four o'clock and the tines centered while the knife is at two o'clock with the tip centered. They form a <. If you must leave the table while the entrée is being eaten and you intend to return and continue eating, leave them in the ^ position with the tines of the fork resting over the tips of the knife.

As I said, there is much disagreement about positioning utensils although we all agree on the relative position of the knife (right for Continental, above for American) and fork (left for Continental, below for American). If you use a variation of these suggestions, please continue to do so. As I said, a little research reveals a variety of suggestions. Regardless of which method you use, do respect the relative positions and keep in mind a couple of other areas of agreement.

One area is you should not lean your utensils against the plate while pausing. The utensil may slip, causing the used utensil to touch the table linens. This guideline has a social etiquette origin and comes to us from a time when most entertaining was done in a private home. In that environment, one avoided soiling the table linens. To do so forced the leader or host to incur an otherwise unnecessary cleaning cost. This was, and is, considered discourteous. Today, social dining often occurs at a public location as does most business dining. Nonetheless, used utensils still should not touch the table linens if for no other reason than to keep your place setting clean and tidy.

Another guideline is to avoid waving the knife and/or fork around while you speak. It is best to rest them, as outlined above, while pausing. This guideline has obvious medieval origins since other diners could consider knife waving an overly aggressive move. At best it is an unnecessary distraction, so rest the utensils when not in use.

Once the entrée (or any course for that matter) is finished, you place your knife and fork in a final position. This position serves two purposes—both focused upon the service or wait staff. One, it signals that you are finished with the course and they can clear your plate. Two, it should make this plate-clearing action effortless and accident-free for the server. This leads to the question: what final position accomplishes these goals?

As mentioned, this is an area of debate in the etiquette community despite general agreement on some basic points. All agree that the knife and fork should be rested side-by-side with the knife above the fork and with the sharp edge facing in. The discussion focuses on two questions: 1. Should you leave the knife and fork at a four o'clock position or a two o'clock position? 2. Should the tines of the fork face down or up?

My recommendation is to leave them

Knife and Forks Finesse

Use
American Style: Start with the knife in your right hand, fork in your left – tines down. Make a cut or two, then rest the knife on the plate and switch fork to your right hand – tines up.

Continental Style: Start in the same manner. Make a cut or two, rest the knife on the plate and keep fork in your left hand - tines down.

Finished Position
1. Rest the knife and fork at a 4 o'clock or 2 o'clock position. I recommend the 2 o'clock to make it easy for the server to secure the utensils while clearing the plate.

2. Leave the tines of the fork facing up; to avoid the irritating scratching sound that can occur when tines are down.

in the two o'clock position with the tines facing up. This simply makes it easier for the server to clear your plate. After spending twenty years in the hospitality business and orchestrating served meals for over 5,000 guests, I know this to be true. We train the wait staff to serve from the left and clear from the right of the guest. This is why we rest the handles of the utensils to the right and why we place them next to each other so the waitperson can grab the plate and secure both utensils with his or her thumb while clearing. I call this move the thumb-lock. This ensures that neither utensil will fall off the plate while being cleared.

I recommend placing the tines of the fork up because this ensures an annoying scratching sound will not be created when the waitperson secures the utensils with his or her thumb. When the tines are down, this thumb-lock move sometimes causes the tips of tines to scrape against the china, creating this abrasive noise. Placing the tines up avoids this outcome.

Whew! As I said, knife and fork usage is an area where consensus about specifics is hard to find. I see this disagreement as a positive since it makes it easy to focus on the conversation when you follow some basic guidelines. The first guideline is to use either the American or the Continental style when cutting. The second is to rest the utensils on the plate when conversing (which you should do often). Third, start and stop eating on pace with the rest of the table. And last, place your utensils so it is easy for the waitperson to clear your plate without incident when finished.

Now let's address two other topics relevant to the entrée: excusing yourself from the table and table talk.

Chapter 16

Excuse Me: Cell Phones and Restrooms

Your goal is to remain seated throughout the entire meal. It is difficult to focus on the business, the conversation, or the relationship when you are away from the table. Still, there are times when you should excuse yourself from the company of others. One such time is when you need to use your cell phone or PDA during a meal. Another, and hopefully obvious, time is when you need to perform a function best done in the privacy of the privy—things like toileting and grooming. I believe there are no exceptions to these guidelines, although some may argue this point. I say you should excuse yourself even when the phone call relates to the topic discussed at the meal or when the bathroom function is simple grooming. Since you may have to excuse yourself from the table during a business meal, we will explore how to do it.

To start, time your departure wisely. Try to do so during a natural pause in the meal service, ideally between courses. Next follow this simple, courteous methodology. Make eye contact with two or three guests (including the leader when he or she is at your table) and say, *"Excuse me."* You need not provide them with the goals of your journey or an agenda of what you hope to accomplish while gone. Just excuse yourself and rise from your chair. Then place your napkin in an acceptable location (as outlined in the next paragraph) and push your chair in so that the aisle behind it remains clear for wait staff and others.

Since you plan to return to the meal, there are two acceptable locations for your napkin. The more traditional placement is to crumple your napkin and rest it on the seat of your chair. The more modern placement is take the napkin, fold it in half so that it mirrors the half-fold used when it rests in your lap, and drape it over the back of your chair. Both indicate that you will be returning to the table.

The modern placement has an interesting social etiquette origin. Years ago, most formal meals occurred in the home or at private clubs. Therefore, the number of *derrières* (rear ends) using a chair was limited, so placing your napkin on the seat of the chair was not an issue. In modern times with most meals occurring in public restaurants, chair usage has increased exponentially. Consequently, hygiene concerns created the modern placement option—draped over the back of the chair—because it eliminates the "derrière contact". The modern placement also shows courtesy to the wait staff as they can easily determine a diner's status from far across the room.

As you know, your goal is to stay at the table so you can engage in conversation and build relationships. Still, some situations dictate that you do leave the table. As stated earlier, the most common reasons to leave the table are to use the cell phone or to visit the restroom. Let me expand on both of these situations, starting with the phone.

Cell phones have created some new and admittedly evolving challenges. I believe it is always discourteous to use a cell phone or to text message when in the company of others. Some argue that it is acceptable to do so when the topic of the call or text relates to the topic at the table; I disagree. While the action may not be disruptive to those at your table, it could be to those dining near you. Disrupting others by making them listen to your end of a private conversation, either spoken or keyed, is discourteous. So in all situations, excuse yourself from the table to take or make a call or text.

When you must receive or make a call/text during the meal, inform the leader and other guests at your table before the meal starts. Be sure the call/text is an absolute necessity, meaning it is either life altering or pertinent to the topic at hand. After being seated, say something like, *"Thank you for dining with me today. I look forward to a memorable meal. However, I do need to tell you that I am expecting a phone call (text message) I will have to receive."* Then put your phone on vibrate (or silent) and store it off the table. Men should keep it in their suit or pants pocket so they can feel the vibration. I suggest that when possible, women do the same. So try to wear something with a pocket if planning to make or receive a call (text). When the call (text) comes in, excuse yourself from the table before answering or reading it.

I also suggest that you excuse yourself to check messages, missed calls, and even the time. When you look at your phone for any reason, you risk saying, *"You are of little significance to me. The person who is on the other end of this phone call (or text message) is much more important to me right now."* This can occur even when checking the time. The people who are observing you don't know what you are doing. They just see your actions and may deduce that the phone is your top priority, not them. I suggest you invest in a wristwatch; it is much easier to check covertly. Just rest your wrist below the surface level of the table and discretely check the time.

The second situation dictating your absence from the

table occurs when you need to visit the restroom. All personal grooming should be done here as well as any function requiring the use of the toilet or sink. Once again, you need not explain where you are going, what you hope to accomplish, or when you plan on returning. Just excuse yourself, place your napkin appropriately, and go take care of your business. Thankfully, almost everyone seems to know this.

Despite such decorum, we sometimes unintentionally announce the need to use the facilities. One such situation occurs when we pass gas, burp, or break wind—to use polite terminology. Yes, I am writing about this topic. After all, everyone does it and often in these dining situations.

Such a release makes sense physiologically. Your body may react differently because business meals often create stress. As a result, the innate "fight or flight" response kicks in. Adrenaline production increases and you are more nervous than usual. All this tension increases gas production and gas release.

The gas has two avenues of escape. It can depart publicly through the mouth or sneak out privately though the rear-exit. It also has a few modes of escape. It might have a slow, lingering, aromatic quality or it might loudly announce its presence in the room. Sometimes, both components exist. These are the deadliest of all!

Regardless of the type of gas released, avenue taken, or mode used, rules of etiquette exist. Before sharing the preferred gas-release etiquette guidelines with you, we will review what you should not do. First, do not blame it on the food. Avoid holding up your plate and saying, *"This fish must be rancid."* We never want to risk embarrassing the leader which such a statement will surely do. Second, do not blame others by saying something like, *"That smells like* one of Robert's. *I think he had tacos for lunch again."* That approach might work at home and it might even work at a business dinner if the goal was to assess blame. As you might guess, that is not the goal.

The goal is twofold, yet simple. Your first goal is keep conversation focused on the business, not the banality of gas release. The second goal is to accept responsibility for your actions. To keep the conversation focused on business, solve the mystery quickly. If no one admits to the error, suspicions arise, curious glances occur, and subtle sniffs of exploration ensue which creates an unproductive table. If the release was overly noxious or loud, neighboring tables might follow suit. Own your error and do it quickly.

A quiet, yet audible, *"Excuse me,"* is sufficient. You need not stand up, extend your arms, and shout, *"It was me."* That is a bit too much. You also need not worry about eye contact, but you do have to speak it loud enough for those around you to hear. Then help keep the table conversation focused on business.

The rationale behind this ownership of your error is, like so many other behaviors, subtle yet significant. When managers and supervisors are asked, *"What qualities do you like your employees to possess?"* one of the most frequent responses is, *"I like people who admit to and take respon-sibility for their mistakes."* Most of us are good at telling others about our accomplishments, about what we have done well. However, few of us are eager to tell others, most particularly our supervisors, about our mistakes. Usually we hope such errors go unnoticed. The problem with this strategy, and I speak from twenty years of experience as a supervisor, is it can lead to embarrassment.

Imagine you are an administrative assistant to a college

dean. One day you mishandle a phone call from the parent of a student. The parent hangs up, irate and threatening to talk to the dean. You decide to go home without telling anyone about the call, hoping the parent was making an idle threat.

The next morning the dean gets a phone call from the customer. "Dr. Knowledge," the parent says. "I know you know what your administrative assistant said to me yesterday. What do you intend to do about this?"

Your dean has few options and ends up saying, "Actually, I don't know what happened. Can I call you back after I get some more information?"

You have placed your supervisor in an awkward and embarrassing situation. It now appears as though she has no idea what goes on in her department. It seems as though she does not have staff trust. You certainly have demonstrated that her staff does not feel comfortable confiding in her either because of fear or lack of respect for her judgment. Bottom line is you have made your boss look bad.

Now imagine the same scenario. You go to your dean and tell her about the mishandled phone call. "Dr. Knowledge," you say, "I think I have mishandled a call today. I want to tell you about it so you can be prepared when and if the parent calls you to complain about my admittedly poor performance. I also want to know how I can better handle such a call correctly the next time I get one."

With this scenario, you have helped your supervisor look good and feel even better. She will look good because she can placate the parent with knowledge and information. This will give the parent confidence in the college. The dean will feel good because you acknowledged her expertise by asking for guidance. Consequently, although it may seem far fetched, acknowledging your gas release suggests that you know how to make your supervisor look good and feel even better.

Perform all other bathroom and grooming related functions in the restroom too. This includes, but is not limited to, coughing, sneezing, teeth picking, and applying lipstick or lip balm (a common business etiquette faux pas).

I understand that many women believe it is acceptable to apply lipstick or lip balm at the table. This misunderstanding occurs because this is true in a social dining environment where gender is a factor. However, as we now know, gender is not a factor in business etiquette (Chapter 13: Business Versus Social Etiquette).

Consequently, I discourage the application of lipstick or lip balm during a business dinner for one simple reason: it screams gender, not professional. Remember your goal is to demonstrate your professional abilities, not your feminine virtues. Applying lipstick defeats this purpose as it says, *"I am woman, see me groom,"* even if only for a moment.

Finally, let me address the sneeze and cough conundrum. Here is where I stray a bit from some of my peers. The old adage was *"never use your napkin as a handkerchief"*. In principle, I agree. You should clearly avoid such use of your napkin. However, what about the worst case scenario? What if I am conversing away, shining through magnificently, and a sneeze suddenly comes upon me? I do not have time to excuse myself and I have not brought a handkerchief with me. Should I really just spew forth into my hands or onto my table mates just so I avoid spoiling the precious linen napkin? Of course not, so here's what I suggest.

When you know you are about to sneeze or cough,

excuse yourself from the table and go to the restroom. If you do not have enough time to leave and must cough at the table, center yourself, lower your head, and cough into your left hand. I know we are now taught to cough into the crook of our elbow. That's a nice idea sometimes, but less pleasant if I am the person seated next you. The left hand is preferred because it is not the hand you use to shake hands and because many cultures consider it the "hygiene" hand. If you do not have enough time to leave and must sneeze at the table without a handkerchief or tissue, center yourself, lower your head, and sneeze into your left hand or your napkin. Sneezes can have a liquid component to them so use the napkin if you sense lots of fluid will be released.

Cough or sneeze as little as possible, avoiding the massive nasal clean-up we sometimes see. Once you are in control, excuse yourself from the table and go to the restroom to wash your hands. If you have used the napkin, carry it with you and deposit it on a bus tray. It is no longer suitable for dinner table use. Trust me when I tell you that guests will appreciate your leaving the table after a cough or sneeze even though you need not announce your intention to scrub your hands.

Chapter 17

Table Talk Tactics

One of our two guiding principles—**it is about the relationship, the conversation, the business; it is not about the food or beverage**—reminds us of the importance of conversation during the meal. Let's discuss the topic of conversation now. There are two distinctive types of conversation that occur during a business meal. The first type of conversation is the "business" or the agenda-driven topic. The other guiding principle—**follow the leader**—reminds us to let the leader initiate this "business" discussion. The second type of conversation is small talk or light conversation. Anyone can initiate small talk.

The "business" discussion usually occurs after entrée service. The reason is quite logical: service staff interruptions are at a minimum. Prior to the arrival of the entrée, all sorts of interruptions occur. We start with greetings made by the leader, guests, and members of the service staff. The service staff follows by announcing specials after which they take food and beverage orders. Then the various preliminary courses are served: beverages, appetizers, soup, dinner rolls, salad, etc. You get the picture. Just when you hunker down to have some serious dialogue, an interruption occurs.

Give the servers your attention, especially early in the meal when reviewing specials and ordering. Remain polite and considerate with servers throughout the meal. Thank them when served if are you not engaged with someone else. Remain still when they serve or clear to reduce the likelihood of an accident. Some business people watch your interactions with service staff closely. Horror stories abound about careers that have been sabotaged because someone got ballistic with a server. This applies even when confronted with poor service. Let the leader address this issue (ideally in private) with management. When others do so, it shows disrespect for the hierarchy. This reaction also embarrasses the leader as if you are saying, *"You not only picked a poor restaurant; you can't manage the situation either."*

As stated, small talk or friendly conversation is on-going. It begins before you even get to the table. This important phase of the dialogue sets the tone for the rest of the meal. Small talk can also be a good icebreaker as it lets others see who you are as a person and how you handle yourself.

One of the best and most overlooked conversational skills is listening. Remember your goal is to engage and connect with the person or people dining with you. Being a good listener is often the best way to do this, especially since people love to talk about themselves and/or their work. Ergo, a great small talk tip is to ask people questions about themselves. Ask questions like, *"What work experiences did you have that best prepared you for your current position?"* or *"How have others in the industry helped you achieve your career success?"* Notice that these questions are open-ended questions, meaning that it takes more than one or two words to answer them. Listening makes people feel significant by showing that you value what they say.

When listening, be active, not passive. Active listeners

remain fully engaged with the person who is speaking. Their facial expressions mirror the content and emotions being shared. Smile when the speaker shares a moment of happiness with you. Reflect empathy when he shares a moment of sorrow. You get the idea—respond, visually and verbally to what is said.

I read recently that one adverse effect of technology, and social networking in particular, is that people do not express empathy as well as they once did. Emoticons do not express empathy. Looking someone in the eye with a comforting expression on your face while saying, *"I understand how frustrated that must have made you feel,"* does.

Another small talk success skill is to know a little about a lot. Your goal is to be able to comment knowledgably about any or most topics presented. This suggestion intimidates some people. They think they need multiple PhDs or that they need a three-story in-home library complete with smoking jacket, pipe, easy chairs, and those cool ladders that roll to the needed section like you see in the movies. Do not be intimidated as this is easier to accomplish than you might suspect.

Table Talk

1. Let the leader initiate the 'business' discussion.
2. Be fully engaged.
3. Actively listen.
4. Be prepared for 'small' talk; set a positive tone.
5. Know a little about a lot.
6. Know what topics to speak about and to avoid.
7. Be polite to servers, while remaining focused on those engaged with.

I have read that if you read three books on any topic or use three trustworthy sites for internet research, you will know more about the topic than 75% of the general population. I believe this to be true. I know that when I read one or two articles about a current event, I know more than most people I speak to that day. So stay current, read a few books, watch some informative television, do some internet research, and you will be able to know a little about a lot. Your goal is follow the topic at hand, whatever it is.

Mastering small talk allows you to demonstrate your interpersonal skills—more specifically, your interpersonal communication skills. Try to appear relaxed and keep the tone positive. Stay neutral and conservative. Make the people you are with feel significant, engaged, and welcome. As stated earlier, you can often achieve this final point by being attentive and speaking about their interests. Lastly, be aware of your volume. Avoid disturbing diners at other tables while being sure that your tablemates don't strain to hear you.

To close this chapter, I will address appropriate and inappropriate conversation topics, focusing more on the inappropriate ones since this is where most errors occur. Appropriate conversation is relatively simple if you remember to stay neutral and conservative. I find that the location—be it the restaurant, catering hall, hotel, neighborhood, city, or state—is always a nice topic. A little preliminary research goes a long way. The arts, sports, human-interest stories, and so on are usually safe as well, especially when you remain neutral.

Another good idea is to do a little research about the individual(s) and/or the organization you are meeting. This should be general information: educational background, new products in development, etc. Don't go all stalker on them. *"I see your middle son is the third baseman for his little league team,"* is a bit too much. *"I saw on LinkedIn that you are a Michigan State graduate. My aunt went there too and she loved it,"* or, *"I read on your company web site that you are entering the Florida market,"* is better. Once the leader brings up the main agenda item, it is clearly appropriate to discuss this as well. Research this more than, but not in lieu of, any other topic.

If you follow the flow of conversation, listen attentively, and comment knowingly every now and then, you should be fine with small talk. As with dining, the goal is to avoid inappropriateness, be it visual or verbal, as it is a distraction. To ensure that you stay on topic, you should know which ones to avoid, especially the "big three" taboo topics.

These are obvious, yet I hear them discussed with surprising frequency. Sexual comments—preferences, desires, history, or observations about the relative "merits" of others—are best kept private. You should also avoid religion with the same caveats. Specific political agendas are best to avoid as well. Of these three, politics is the toughest to avoid. I suggest expressing neutral, middle-of-the-road opinions as much as possible. Leaning too far right or too far left can be troublesome. Finally, when complimenting someone, compliment professional skills and performance only. Personal compliments are always unacceptable. *"That was a wonderful presentation,"* is acceptable. *"You look incredibly sexy in that business suit,"* is not.

Once the "business" discussion occurs, conversation gets easier. Remain fully engaged with the person or people at your table. Arrive prepared so you can focus on the agenda and contribute to the conversational flow and content. Answer questions honestly, remembering what you promise to do. Follow through on promises made. Ask questions when appropriate, after permitting the speaker to finish.

Let me remind you once again that your goal is to **let you shine though**. Table talk is how you accomplish this. Communicate what is great, wonderful, unique, and special about you. Do so in a manner that makes others feel significant and engaged. Remember being an attentive listener is a desirable skill. Avoid the distraction of inappropriate behavior and inappropriate topics and you will **shine while you dine**.

SECTION FIVE:

Closing the Meal, Sealing the Deal

Chapter 18

Dessert Dexterity

Dessert, if served, follows the entrée. It provides symbolic and culinary closure to the meal. Nonetheless, it is an optional course even when served at a banquet. If you are not interested, simply say, *"None for me, thank you."* It is a course often skipped at lunch since time is a concern. When served, it is important to enjoy it appropriately.

When using a basic table setting (one knife, one fork, and one spoon for example), the correct utensil will be served when and if you order dessert. At a more formal setting, you may see a fork, a spoon, or both set at the top of the place setting. Unless the spoon is a soup spoon, they are most likely dessert utensils. If so, leave them there until they serve dessert.

Once dessert is served to everyone at the table, slide the utensil(s) into the appropriate position—fork to the left of the dessert plate, spoon to the right. Once everyone at the table has slid his utensil(s) into this position, you can enjoy your dessert. Avoid picking the utensil(s) up directly from the top of the place setting. Always slide them into position first. Note too that the service staff may slide them down for you. I suggest you wait a moment after the dessert plate is set in front of you before sliding them into position. Once it's clear the staff will not do this and everyone else is served, do the "utensil slide".

Cut (or break when appropriate) and eat one piece of dessert at a time. If served only a spoon, use the spoon to cut a bite at a time, then lift it to your lips. If served only a fork, use the fork to cut a bite a time, then lift it to your lips. Since some desserts have a high potential for crumb creation, like pastries and piecrusts, both a spoon and a fork might be set. When both a dessert spoon and dessert fork are set, slide them into position (let the handles lead the way), use the fork to cut and the spoon to lift the bite to your lips. The spoon is used for lifting to minimize the quantity of crumbs that fall.

It is a common social practice to share dessert. Despite the popularity of this custom, I would avoid initiating it at a business meal. When others are insistent, especially the leader, you can follow suit. When you share dessert or any food, remember to ask for a second plate. Place some of dessert on your plate (with unused utensils) and eat from your plate, not theirs.

If all has gone well during the meal (and it did if you have adhered to the two guiding principles), **you have shown through**! I say, "Bravo and congratulations for a job well done." The last impression is often the lasting impression, so stay focused even as the meal winds down. Continue to follow (or be) the leader and remember that it is about the relationship, the conversation, and the business; it is not about the food or beverage.

Chapter 19

Coffee & Tea......Finally!

A question often asked during my seminars is, *"When is the proper time for one to enjoy coffee or tea?"* The quick and easy answer is when it is offered. I know that some consider it impolite to enjoy coffee or tea during the entrée. They feel these are after-dinner or dessert beverages. While I am sensitive to these feelings, I respect the hierarchy—meaning the leader decides when to offer and serve everything, including the coffee and tea. If it is offered during the entrée, feel comfortable accepting it. However, be aware that you might offend some at the table so you may want to err on the side of caution and wait for dessert.

Regardless of when the coffee and tea appears on the table, keep a few things in mind. The first is to initiate passing whether you are having a cup or not. If the sugar, sweetener, cream, or lemon is set nearest you, pick it up and pass it to the person to your right saying, *"Would you care for some sugar?"* Remember the initiator does not take any at this time. If possible, you may first offer some to the person to your left (provided you keep hold of the bowl or saucer) then pass to the right.

After supplementing your beverage, stir the liquid—not the cup. Stirring should be silent. Tea connoisseurs suggest you add sugar first and then let it dissolve before adding the lemon. Adding the lemon first hinders the ability of the sugar to dissolve.

Avoid resting used items on the table; this might soil the linens. Rest your teaspoon on the saucer after use. Place used creamer pc's (short for portion control) there too or on your bread and butter plate if still available. Avoid returning them to the common pc plate or bowl because of the dribble potential. I assess the options before using a pc at a dinner. If I see no convenient place to rest the used pc, I either pass on the coffee or drink it black. Remember it is about the relationships, not about the food or beverage.

You can tuck used sugar or sweetener packets under your saucer and/or bread and butter plate. Since they are a powder rather than a liquid, they will not soil the linens. Lemons should remain in the beverage or resting upon the saucer/bread and butter plate. You should remove tea bags from the beverage. Rest them in the same location.

Remember to sip—don't slurp—just like with soup but without the use of the spoon! Finally, if you do not want coffee or tea when offered, just wave your hand over your cup and say, *"None for me, thanks,"* as opposed to turning your cup upside down.

Now to the most important beverage questions: *"Is it acceptable to drink alcohol at a business meal?"* and *"If so, how much?"*

Chapter 20

To Drink (Alcohol) or Not to Drink?
That Is the Question

The most common question asked at my seminars concerns alcohol consumption at a business dinner. Sometimes it seems they want me to say, *"Go ahead, continue to order three Manhattans and regale the interviewer with your raucous charm and bawdy sense of humor. That certainly cannot be why you were passed over for the last promotion."* Much to their chagrin, I do not say this.

Instead, I suggest you refrain from drinking alcohol at a business dinner, especially when first being introduced to an organization and its culture or at an interview. Once familiar with an organization and its culture, you may enjoy an alcoholic beverage or two if the corporate culture accepts this, but always drink in moderation. It is best to err on the side of sobriety. Often a series of "what if" questions follow my recommendation. I will address these at the end of this chapter. Before I do that, let me explain why I suggest you start with restraint and abstinence.

First of all, remember that your single most important goal during a business meal is **to shine while you dine**. You best achieve this when sober because your talents, creativity, personality, and unique and wonderful qualities are fully displayed. When you start drinking alcohol, you are no longer at your best. Some of us think we are even better than our best when drinking; this is a myth. If you haven't learned that yet, you will (hopefully). Maintaining the ability to remain at our best is reason enough to abstain or, at the very least, show restraint.

Remember also alcohol may affect you differently at such a meal. Your nervous system may be on red-alert, especially if it is an interview situation. The "flight-or-fight" syndrome may kick in, causing hormones to be released into your body. As a result, what you can comfortably drink on a Friday night out with friends may hit you differently, meaning more quickly and harder.

Years ago a co-worker and I used to go out every Thursday night after work. He would have four pints of Guinness and I would have four pints of Labatt's Blue. He was what is often called a "good drunk", meaning I couldn't even tell he had been drinking. Of course, I had four Blues in me so my judgment might have been slightly impaired. Still, he handled his liquor well. Then he went for a job interview. It was a job he wanted very much as it involved a pay raise and a desired relocation. When he returned from the interview, he had a long, sad face. I could tell the interview had not gone well.

"How did the interview go?" I asked, fearful of the response.

"I think I blew it," he replied.

"Why, what happened?" I inquired.

"I had some beer, half a bottle of Heineken to be exact, and it hit me—hard. I think it was because I was so nervous. I felt myself grinning uncontrollably. Then I laughed at an inappropriate time. This made me even more nervous. I was off, just off."

Sure enough, he did not get the job offer he had wanted. He had blown this once in a lifetime opportunity all because he had decided to have a drink.

Another reason was revealed to me a few years back. I was presenting a dining etiquette seminar for a university's career services department. They invited three or four potential employers to the event to meet and mingle with the eighty-plus students in attendance. After discussing the wisdom of abstinence (especially during an interview), one of the employers asked this question:

"What if I ordered a bottle of wine for the table? Wouldn't it be rude for someone to decline?"

I gave my usual response and stated that since alcohol consumption is a personal decision, I suggested he decline if it was an interview or he was just learning the corporate culture. To do so he would simply pass or wave his hand over his wine glass and say, *"None for me,"* when offered. Once he was familiar with the culture, I continued that he may feel comfortable enjoying a glass or two. Until then, it is better to err on the side of abstinence.

After the event, I approached the employer who asked the question. My suspicion was that he had asked this question with a specific response in mind.

"Was that the answer you wanted?" I asked.

"That was the exact answer I wanted," he replied. *"I work for a major pharmaceutical company and we do it as a test."*

This is not to say that everyone who declined the glass of wine was hired, or that everyone who accepted was not.

It was not the determining factor, but it WAS a factor. That's what you should keep in mind. Human Resources experts agree that the number one cause of all employee-related problems is substance abuse, so why display a potentially disruptive and expensive characteristic to a potential employer?

My recommendation of abstinence is strongest when engaged in initial interviews (be they for a job, sale, or promotion) and when you first begin working for an organization. Once you get to know the culture, you may decide to drink in moderation if it appears to be part of the corporate culture. When doing so, keep a few things in mind.

The most important thing to remember is the single most important goal – **to let you shine through**. Your purpose is to take this opportunity to once again demonstrate your unique, creative, and wonderful assets. Hopefully being a "fun" or "happy" drunk is not one of your special skills. In business situations, moderation really means moderation. So when the culture permits, enjoy a drink or two if you can handle your alcohol. The idea is to blend in and shine through, not to get drunk. It is not about the food or the beverage!

If you do decide to drink in moderation and your drink of choice is beer, consider choosing otherwise. Drinking beer, especially when consumed directly from the bottle or can, may communicate an inappropriate casualness. Arguably, some events are more appropriate for beer than others such as company picnics, ballgames, and golf outings. Even at these events, drink in moderation and drink from a glass or cup.

At more formal events, steer clear of beer because it makes you appear too casual. Spirits such as vodka, gin, and whiskey are other options; however, they are the most powerful options so chose them with great caution. Consequently, wine may be the best choice.

When wine is selected, you will decide between a red and white wine. Most often this means a room temperature or a chilled beverage. Temperature matters because it dictates how you should hold the wine glass. When enjoying a red wine or room temperature beverage (i.e. brandy), hold the stemmed glass by the bowl. This ensures the quality of the beverage will be maintained as the temperature of your palm warms the beverage.

Conversely, when enjoying a white or chilled beverage (i.e. champagne), hold the glass by the stem, not the bowl. If you hold a white wine glass by the bowl, your palm warms the beverage, deteriorating its quality. Hold it by the stem instead to let the beverage remain chilled as intended. Holding a chilled beverage by the stem has the additional benefit of avoiding condensation on your hand.

Chilled beverages create condensation on the bowl. This moisture gets transferred to your hand when held by the bowl, leading to a clammy, awkward handshake. For this reason, hold your beverage in your left hand when min-gling. This leaves your right hand free for the all-important handshake. Professionals who do a lot of networking learn to hold their appetizer plate in their left hand too. That's right—they carry their appetizer plate <u>and</u> their beverage glass in their left hand while working the room. You can do this too.

Start by placing a cocktail napkin between the little finger and ring finger of your left hand. Then tilt your hand so that is palm-up as if someone is going to "slap you five". Rest the appetizer plate on your palm, little finger, ring finger, and middle finger—securing it with your pointer. The pointer, or index finger, sits atop the plate and the rest sit below. Take your glass and hold it with your index finger and thumb, resting the bottom of the glass or stem on the edge of your appetizer plate. This will come easily to you with a little practice. Your right hand is now free to shake hands, take a drink, or nibble on an appetizer. If a little moisture or some crumbs get on your fingertips, discreetly wipe them on your cocktail napkin.

Remember your right hand is your power hand. I believe that you will meet a limited number of people who can have a positive impact upon your career. Having your right hand free ensures the first contact with this person will be positive, possibly setting the stage for the wonders that may follow. If this first contact is not positive, you may be left with one less opportunity. Clammy hands kill opportunities.

A last tip regarding this maneuver is to look for people who are adept at holding their appetizer plate and beverage in their left hand. Chances are they are experienced at networking so even if you are a network novice approach these people. You can even say, *"I see this isn't your first conference. It is mine. I wonder if you have any tips you'd be willing to share with me so I can look as comfortable as you do."*

Let me answer a few of the most commonly asked alcohol-related questions. The first is, *"If you decide to drink alcohol once you know the culture, what do you choose?"* Most often, I select wine as recommended. However, I do have a fall back—scotch. I make this decision based upon what others are selecting. I like scotch for a couple of reasons. The first is that I cannot drink it quickly. I do not do shots and could not with scotch. I find this is helpful if I am more nervous than usual. Early in my career I found that when I selected wine or beer, I would drink two or three fairly quickly, meaning I could no longer shine though.

For me, scotch is a slow-sipping beverage. One glass can last a couple of hours. If I do need to refill, I just top it off with some water. This way I look distinguished and limit my alcohol intake.

A second question is, *"What if I go out with my co-workers for happy hour? Isn't that a social situation, meaning I can get a little drunk?"* If your career could be impacted by your words, actions, or behaviors, then it is a professional situation; therefore, I recommend moderation or abstinence. This may be the most important question asked today because of the internet and cell phone technology. Just open your favorite social networking site and you will see millions of pictures of people in compromising positions. No permission is required to take a pic of you while crooning out your favorite song while shirtless, drunk, and sloppy. No permission is required for someone to post it on the net. No permission is required for your boss or potential employer to view it. If you'd be embarrassed if they'd see it, don't do it.

A final question is, *"I've worked with this culture and getting drunk is part of the culture. Aren't I obligated to do so in this situation?"* Once again and as always, I preach moderation or abstinence for the reasons outlined earlier. A story told to me after a seminar best explains why.

It was told by a woman who had been the first female senior vice-president of a major company. I won't mention the industry, but she related that the other vice-presidents had a long history of heavy drinking bouts, especially at conferences, trade shows, after board meetings, etc. She felt the need to participate in these sessions to fit in and be accepted as a peer; however, she wanted to be at her best and did not want to drink. Her solution was brilliant.

She would join them in the lounge, tavern, or bar, but not before stopping to speak with the bartender or server. She instructed the wait staff to serve her only soda water, regardless of what she ordered. So while her peers saw her ordering multiple vodka tonics, she was drinking multiple soda waters with a lime garnish. As a result, she blended in and helped permanently shatter the glass ceiling for her industry.

This example proves once again that it really is about the relationship, the conversation, the business; it is not about the food or the beverage—especially when the beverage is alcohol. Moderation, if not abstinence, is always the best path to follow.

Chapter 21

Depart with Dignity

Finally, the end of the meal is at hand. With this in mind, remember that *"the last impression leaves a lasting impression"*. Your goal is to close the meal as effectively as you opened it. In a restaurant, you will know the meal is coming to a close when the check is presented. This moment often causes the greatest consternation among novice business diners. Questions fill their head: *"Who pays the check? Should I offer to pay half? Should I cover the tip if another pays?"*

The guideline here is relatively simple and surprisingly well-understood. It can be adhered to once again by **following the leader**. The person who does the inviting (the leader) pays the bill. This is a time-honored maxim in most fields, especially when there is a clear superior-subordinate relationship. The interviewer pays for the interviewee. The boss pays for the subordinate after discussing a possible promotion. In these scenarios, it is invariably the interviewer or the superior who initiates the meal invitation. Note that this guideline is most often followed when two things occur. The first is that the meal has a business focus and the second is that an invitation has been extended and accepted.

There are some variations, most notably if you work in politics or with government employees. Regulations often prohibit the acceptance of gifts in these fields and a meal may be construed as a gift. In such situations, each diner typically pays for their own meal.

Another variation occurs when the meal has a social focus despite an aura of business. This most often occurs when a group of co-workers decides to eat lunch together. While business may be discussed (often in the form of a "gripe" session, to use a polite term), there is not a clear business agenda. In these situations, it is often easiest to split the bill evenly or ask for separate checks before ordering.

At large events, payment is pre-arranged so this is not an issue. Still, the guideline is followed. The group that does the inviting pays the bill. Payment is pre-arranged and no check is presented. I doubt you feel obligated to offer to pay the bill at a national conference dinner or even leave a tip. You need not feel obligated when accepting a more personal dinner invitation either.

However, when you dine frequently with someone, do try to reciprocate his kindness. Let's say you are invited to meal by someone who wants to engage your services as a consultant. Since she did the inviting, she is the leader and you let her pay the bill. If it is clear that a second meal is required, make sure that you invite her, which makes you the leader the next time. You can do this while exiting the first meal if you like. *"Thanks so much for this chance to speak with you. This is such a wonderful restaurant,"* you might start. Then continue, *"Can you join me for dinner next week so that we can continue our discussion? I can give you call later this week to work out the time and location."*

This guideline—the inviter pays—often applies socially as well, even when entertaining in one's home. Even today, accepting an invitation to a social dinner party at someone's private home implies two things. One is that you will attend the dinner. The second is that you will reciprocate this kindness (usually within a year) by extending an invitation to a dinner party that you host. Admittedly, this guideline is often ignored, making it a powerful gesture when followed. Regardless of its frequency of practice, it confirms the point—the inviter pays.

The leader also determines when the meal is finished. This may be done verbally or non-verbally. The simple statement, *"It looks like we're done here,"* is sufficient. This message can also be communicated non-verbally when the leader rises from his seat which he should be the first to do.

When rising from the table at the end of the meal, napkin placement comes into play for the final time. Remember it has remained in your lap throughout the meal. When in use, you have lifted it to your lips and blotted gently. If you had to excuse yourself from the table during the meal (which you tried to avoid if possible), you either placed it on the seat of your chair or draped it over the back of your chair. Upon your return to the table, you placed it in your lap once again. Now that the meal is done, it is time to place the used napkin in its final position.

Departing with Dignity

1. The leader indicates when the meal is done.
2. Your napkin is crumpled and placed on the table.
3. The leader pays.*
4. Thank you, times two.

* Unless prohibited by industry guidelines.

This is another area of some debate in the etiquette world. We all agree that the used napkin should be crumpled and placed on the table to signify that you are done. We disagree on where exactly is should be placed. Some of us say it should be placed to the left of our original place setting, some say it should be placed to the right of our original place setting, and others say it should be placed in the center. Which is it: left, right, or center?

After much thought and inquiry, I suggest that you place it where you originally found it at the table. If your napkin was set to the left, leave it on the left. If your napkin was set to the right (often in an empty wine or water glass), leave it on the right. If your napkin was set in the center (perhaps on your cover plate), leave it in the center.

I've concluded that this is the best answer because I believe it mirrors the true intent of this action. The practice of leaving the crumpled napkin on the table when the meal is done has a social origin. When I was young, my grandmother taught me to leave my crumpled napkin on the left side of my place setting because this is where my napkin in its own napkin ring had been set at the start of the meal. When I met people who preferred a right-placement, I learned that their napkin and napkin ring were set to the right. When I met people who preferred a center-placement, I learned that—you guessed it—their napkin and napkin ring were pre-set in the center of their place setting. Clearly, the intent was to place the hopefully unsoiled napkin back in the ring so it could be re-used at the next meal.

Think back to the early days of social dining in America when travel was a time-consuming affair. If I spent days traveling to someone's house, I would not stay for one night. A prolonged visit was the norm and sometimes lasted up to a month; consequently, I would attend multiple meals. Courtesy dictated that when I did so, I would re-use my napkin as much as possible so that the host (or leader) would not incur the additional expense of providing me with a clean one. The goal is to place your napkin so that it can be identified for re-use if possible.

This does not mean that restaurants re-use napkins; they do not. Fresh linens are the norm so we no longer do this to ensure proper re-use. Nonetheless, I suggest ending the meal by placing the used napkin near the place it was set at the beginning of the meal. It was courteous long ago and remains courteous even today.

The final key to departing with dignity is to remember to say thank you times two. This principle has two specific applications: the first regarding what you thank the leader for, the second concerning the media used to express your gratitude.

You start by saying thank you while exiting the restaurant or the event. Thank the leader for two things: the conversation AND the meal. *"Thank you so much for the opportunity to meet with you today,"* you can begin. Then add, *"You picked a wonderful restaurant. The food and service were excellent."* This simple statement accomplishes many things. You confirm your awareness that the most important component of the meal was the conversation, the relationship, the business—not the food or beverage. While this is indeed true, you also want to express appreciation for the food and beverage; acts of hospitality always deserve gratitude. Finally, you subtly compliment the leader's decision making ability. After all, he did decide on where to dine and a little flattery can go a long way.

An e-mail thank you can then be sent. I would avoid a text message thank you because it may appear too personal and consequently unprofessional. Just keep in mind that an e-mail thank you may not even be read. At one point in my career, I sometimes received over 300 e-mails each day. I quickly developed a "quick edit" mentality to weed out the unnecessary correspondence. A subject line that says "thank you" was one of the first to go. I already knew what the message said so why read it?

The most effective thank you is the hand-written thank you note or card that you mail through the United States Postal Service within a week of the meal. You send a hand-written note so that it is physically held when it is read. This tactile action increases retention; I've read many reports confirming this. When you hold a document in your hands while reading it, you remember the content better and for a longer time than if you read it off a computer monitor or LCD display. A hand-written thank you note for the conversation and the meal ensures that you will be remembered.

Chapter 22

Final Thought

You now have the tools needed to **shine while you dine**. Keep your focus on your single goal. Use the two guiding principles to negotiate your way through any unfamiliar situations. Know that your actions are built upon the three foundations of all appropriate behavior. It really is as easy as one-two-three.

So relax and embrace all that is wonderful, unique, special, talented, and creative about you. I am certain there is much to embrace. Use the skills outlined in this book to best bring them to your profession and to our world.

Made in the USA
San Bernardino, CA
03 May 2016